Timnah

Cover: Aerial view of Tel Batash (Timnah). (Photo by Richard Cleave.)

Timnah

A Biblical City in the Sorek Valley

George L. Kelm
and
Amihai Mazar

Winona Lake, Indiana
Eisenbrauns
1995

Scripture quotations are from the Revised Standard Version,
© copyright The National Council of Churches,
used by permission.

Library of Congress Cataloging in Publication Data

Kelm, George L., 1931–
    Timnah : a biblical city in the Sorek Valley / George L. Kelm and Amihai
Mazar.
        p.   cm.
    Includes bibliographical references.
    ISBN 0-931464-97-8
    1. Timna Site (Israel) 2. Excavations (Archaeology)—Israel.
I. Mazar, Amihay, 1942–   . II. Title.
DS110.T63K45 1995
933—dc20   95-21534
                                                        CIP

The paper used in this publication meets the minimum requirements of the American
National Standard for Information Sciences—Permanence of Paper for Printed Library
Materials, ANSI Z39.48-1984. ⊗ ™

Acknowledgment

This volume honors

Mary D. and F. Howard Walsh

who have facilitated the Timnah expedition's contribution to biblical and archaeological research by sponsoring its publication. Their personal interest and financial generosity is most gratefully appreciated.

Contents

Abbreviations

List of Tables

List of Figures

List of Color Figures

Samson went down to Timnah . . . (Judg 14:1)

The romance, intrigue, frustration, and ultimate desperation of the Israelite judge Samson in his valiant attempts at claiming his tribe's inheritance in the Promised Land is well known to every Bible student. The geographical focus of Samson's exploits in the biblical narratives is primarily on Timnah and its environs. Its location was within the strategic buffer zone between the militarily superior Philistines and their weaker Israelite neighbors in the rugged Judean hill country to the east. Efforts by Samson and his Danite kinsmen to move into the productive valleys of the Shephelah and the fertile coastal plain highlighted only one period in an extended series of critical military and economic struggles in which the town identified with Tel Batash played a dominant role throughout its long and colorful history. Its obvious strategic location and the possible clarification of its unique political and commercial role in the northern Shephelah prompted the selection of the site for our projected long-term excavation project.

I have a vivid recollection of the first time we *went down to Timnah.* It was during our first visit to Israel in 1960, when Lin and I were students at the Institute of Holy Land Studies in Jerusalem. The primary focus of our academic program was the land of Israel, its topography, geography, archaeology and history, complemented by on-site study of important biblical town sites. A field trip to the Shephelah brought us along the Sorek Valley. While photographing the distinctive square mound of Tel Batash and the surrounding terrain, I recall thinking, "Wouldn't this be a perfect site to excavate?"

During the next fifteen years, additional opportunities to visit and pass by the site always renewed the intrigue of Samson's exploits and stimulated the growing desire to know more of its history. On occasion we even expressed the dream of actually excavating the site to the individuals or groups we had the opportunity of guiding through the area.

Ultimately, after archaeological field experience at other sites (Har Yeruham, Tel Malhata, and five years in an intensive supervisory role at Tel Aphek-Antipatris), we felt the need for an archaeological field school involved in the excavation of a biblical site in which the students and volunteers we recruited, most with a distinct biblical orientation, could find more meaningful fulfillment of their special academic and vocational objectives.

My own Aphek experience had identified two historical periods that were of special personal interest and concern. During three seasons of supervising the excavation of its Late Bronze strata, that interest had been focused on the complexities of the Late Bronze–Iron Age transition, the decline of the Canaanite culture, and the possible biblical correlations of the simultaneous Israelite and Philistine settlements in Canaan and the subsequent conflict along their mutual borders. When we later sought a potential site for an independently sponsored excavation, these important factors tended to guide our evaluation and the ultimate selection of Tel Batash.

Obviously, for an educational program primarily sponsored by New Orleans Baptist Theological Seminary where I was teaching at the time, a site of biblical significance was viewed as having greater appeal for the recruitment of volunteers not only among the student body but among the wider seminary constituency as well. Following an extensive survey of the northern Philistine coastal plain and Shephelah and the personal advice and wise counsel of our friend, Professor Benjamin Mazar, we requested permission from the Israel Department of Antiquities and Museums to excavate Tel Batash. It is my hope that in this volume we have been able to convey some of the excitement and scope of our excavation experiences during our twelve seasons on the site. Throughout the entire course of the project I have enjoyed a very warm and cordial professional relationship with my colleague Amihai Mazar. It has been a rewarding friendship for which I always will be grateful.

During the twelve seasons of our excavations at Tel Batash (Timnah) the field work, together with its complementary academic and travel program, provided an excellent educational adventure for its staff and volunteers. This volume is dedicated primarily to approximately six hundred dedicated, hard-working volunteers who during those twelve years, individually and collectively, achieved the results that are partly recorded here. This volume, based on our three preliminary reports of the excavations (*BASOR* 248; *BASOR Supplement* 23, *BASOR Supplement* 27) and subsequent study, is intended to express gratitude to them and to other immediate friends of the project who assisted financially; and it is also designed for a wider audience, for whom the final excavation reports will be either unavailable or too technical. We trust that the initial aspirations and objectives of the program for enhancing a broader understanding of archaeological contributions to biblical studies will be served by this volume.

George L. Kelm

1 Tel Batash: The Site and Its Identification

Tel Batash (Israel map reference 1416.1325) is located on the fertile alluvial Sorek Plain in the northern Shephelah. This plain, bordered on the north and south by ridges of chalky limestone hills, slopes gently northwestward from Beth-Shemesh at the base of the Judean Hills. The Brook Sorek (Wadi Sarar) meanders along the kilometer-wide plain, providing a perennial water source for the ancient town site located on its southern bank. Thanks to its central location in the plain, the town controlled this natural corridor from the coastal plain to the strategic passes to Bethlehem and Jerusalem on the Judean watershed and the vital north–south road along the western base of the Judean Hills. There, gentle undulating terrain provided easy access to the strategic towns in the interior of the southern Shephelah.

The history of the site was linked to the development of three other cities in the region: Beth-Shemesh (7 km to the southeast), Gezer (8 km to the north), and Tel Miqne-Ekron (6 km to the west). The central plain around the mound provided abundant land for agriculture and grazing, while springs along the Sorek Valley and shallow wells dug down to the relatively high water table along its banks provided a sufficient water supply. The area also enjoyed an adequate annual rainfall of about 450 mm.

This ideal agricultural setting, its proximity to a primary road linking the coastal plain with the central hill country, and even the square shape of the mound were physical

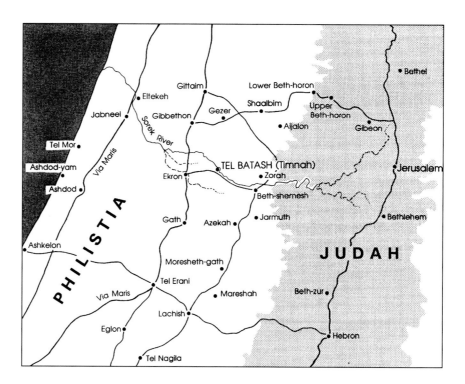

Fig. 1.1. Map of Northern Shephelah, with location of Tel Batash (Timnah) in the Sorek Valley.

attributes that significantly contributed to the site's development as a strategic urban center. The tell, a distinctive 200 × 200 m square with its sides oriented to the points of the compass, covers 40 dunams (10 acres) at its base. The upper surface of the tell (150 × 150 m, approximately 22.5 dunams or 5.6 acres) is concave and rises 12 to 15 meters or about 40 feet above the surrounding plain. The highest point (131 m above sea level), located in the northeastern quadrant, dominated a terrace that apparently extended to the bank of the Sorek. The slopes of the tell are uniformly steep, evidence of the massive earthen ramparts that determined the mound's original shape and outer limits and provided the foundation for subsequent defensive systems. Aerial photographs and a field survey facilitated the identification of the remnants of the latest fortification system, including the location of its gate complex near the center of the eastern slope.

Earlier Geographical Research

The first mention of Tel Batash in modern geographical research came from a French pioneer in biblical archaeology,

Fig. 1.2. Aerial view of Tel Batash in the alluvial Sorek Plain.

Charles Clermont-Ganneau, who visited the site in 1871 during his search for ancient Gezer in the northern Shephelah.[1] While following the Sorek Valley, he recorded his discovery of a square mound named *Tell el-Batasheh* (according to his transcription; on older maps the Arabic name of the site usually appears as Tell el-Batashi or Butashi, Tel Batash in modern Hebrew). Without the benefit of dating skills based on ceramic evidence, Clermont-Ganneau surmised from the shape of the mound that the site had been a Roman or Byzantine military camp or fortress.

Over a century of biblical research passed without any significant study of this important mound. However, during the early 1940s, the tell was surveyed by B. Mazar and J. Kaplan, who identified it as an important Iron Age site. Though Kaplan later discovered Neolithic, Chalcolithic, and Middle Bronze II remains at nearby Teluliot Batashi,[2] the tell itself remained untouched. As recent as 1959, its importance was still entirely overlooked in important publications on the historical geography of the Shephelah.[3] In 1976, surveys of the mound and its vicinity were conducted by Z. Kallai and A. Mazar with students from the Institute of Archaeology of The Hebrew University of Jerusalem. Late Bronze and Iron Age pottery was recovered, the Iron Age city wall along the mound's crest was identified, and it was hypothesized that the distinctive shape of the tell had been established and maintained by Middle Bronze ramparts buried along its perimeter.

The Identification of Tel Batash with Biblical Timnah

The earliest biblical reference to Timnah occurs in the patriarchal narrative concerning Judah's encounter with Tamar while on his way to Timnah to shear his sheep (Gen 38:12–14). Their son Perez later appears in the lineage of King David. The narrative also refers to Adullam, Kezib, and other Canaanite cities in the Shephelah that apparently were located in the vicinity of Timnah.

The most important source for the identification of Tel Batash with Timnah is the biblical description of the northern border of Judah's tribal area (Josh 15:10–11). The east-to-west border description in the Judean Hills is followed by details of the boundary in the Shephelah:

> . . . [the boundary] goes down to Beth-Shemesh, and passes along by Timnah; the boundary goes out to the shoulder of the hill north of Ekron . . .

This biblical passage locates Timnah between Beth-Shemesh and Ekron. Early geographical studies of the region had erroneously identified Timnah with Khirbet Tibneh (Tabaneh), east of Adullam (Sheikh Madkur) on a lower ridge of the Judean Hills and 5 km southeast of Tel Batash,[4] and scholars generally agreed that the name "Tibneh" preserved the ancient biblical name *Timnah*. On this basis, B. Mazar proposed that biblical Ekron should be identified with Tel Batash,[5] rather than with Qatra (much farther to the west), as suggested by Albright.[6]

A dramatic breakthrough occurred in 1956, when J. Naveh discovered the lower city of Khirbet el-Muqannah (Hebrew: Tel Miqne) and suggested that this large mound should be identified with Ekron.[7] His insight logically led to the Tel Batash = Timnah equation, since this was the only mound of any significance between Beth-Shemesh and Tel Miqne (Ekron). In spite of Albright's opposition, these identifications soon were generally accepted.[8] Most scholars recognized that the new identifications of Ekron and Timnah contributed to a clearer understanding of Israel's tribal boundaries and of the territorial limits of the kingdom of Ekron.[9]

In our opinion, the Timnah mentioned in Genesis 18 is identical with the Timnah of the boundary descriptions in Josh 15:10–11 and is to be located at Tel Batash. The discovery of a prosperous Canaanite city at Tel Batash tends to support this identification. Some scholars have interpreted the narrative in Genesis 38 as reflecting the peaceful penetration of the tribe of Judah into the northern Shephelah, a region that is not mentioned in the conquest narrative recorded in the book of Joshua.[10]

Most of the events in the life of Samson took place in the vicinity of Timnah (Judges 14–15). According to the biblical narrative, the Philistines, with superior strength, controlled Timnah and the Sorek Valley and frustrated any attempts by the tribes of Judah and Dan to extend their western frontier.

Timnah's fate during the United Monarchy is relatively obscure. It may have come under Israelite control during David's westward expansion into the northern Shephelah and the region of Jaffa. It is mentioned as *Timnathah* in the list of Danite cities (Josh 19:43). According to B. Mazar, its inclusion in this list reflects Israelite territorial expansion during the United Monarchy.[12] Its placement in the list between Eilon and Ekron and following the more easterly cities (Zorah, Eshtaol, Beth-Shemesh, Shaalbim and Yitlah) tends to support its identification with Tel Batash. After the division of the kingdom, the region may have reverted to Philistine control. It may be significant that Timnah is not mentioned among the cities fortified by Rehoboam (2 Chr 11:3–11). Although his primary line of defense passed through Azekah, Adullam, Zorah, and Aijalon, farther to the east, the question remains whether this list marks the border of Judah during his reign, or whether the actual border was located farther to the west, encompassing Timnah.[13] Timnah may have been rebuilt as a Judean town after Uzziah's reconquest of the region and his western expansion of Judean territory at Philistia's expense (2 Chr 26:6). Timnah and other cities in the northern Shephelah were reclaimed by the Philistines during the reign of Ahaz (2 Chr 28:18), and once again may have become a part of the kingdom of Ekron.

The final historical reference to Timnah is related to Sennacherib's invasion of Judah during the reign of Hezekiah.[14] After occupying the territories of Ashkelon along the Yarkon River, Sennacherib moved against Ekron which was temporarily under Hezekiah's control. According to Sennacherib's annals, two battles preceded the taking of Ekron: the battle of Eltekeh, where the Assyrians disposed of a token Egyptian force sent to assist the rebels, and the conquest of Timnah. The mention of the conquest of Timnah in the context of the war against Ekron seems to imply a relationship between the two. As we shall see, the excavations at Tel Batash have produced direct evidence of this confrontation.

The archaeological investigations at Tel Batash have demonstrated that the town flourished during the seventh century B.C.E. until it was destroyed in a massive conflagration ca. 600 B.C.E. Timnah is not mentioned, however, in any of the written sources from this century. One of the major questions concerning this period, therefore, is whether the town was under Ekron's control, or whether it belonged to the kingdom of Judah under Manasseh and Josiah.

Endnotes

1. Ch. Clermont-Ganneau, *Archaeological Researches in Palestine*, (London: Palestine Exploration Fund, 1896) vol. 2, 466.

2. J. Kaplan, "Excavations at Teluliot Batashi in the Vale of Sorek," *Eretz-Israel* 5 (1958) 9–24 (Hebrew).

3. For example, J. Simons, *The Geographical and Topographical Texts of the Old Testament* (Leiden: Brill, 1959); Simons does not mention the site at all.

4. See W. F. Albright, "Topographical Researches in Judaea." *BASOR* 18 (1925) 10; F.-M. Abel, *Geographie de la Palestine* (Paris: Gabalda, 1938) vol. 2, 481; J. Simons, *Geographical and Topographical Texts*, 141, 371.

5. B. Mazar, "The Campaign of Sennacherib in Judea," *Eretz-Israel* 2 (1953) 171 (Hebrew).

6. W. F. Albright, "Contributions to the Historical Geography of Palestine 1: The Sites of Ekron, Gath and Libnah," *AASOR* 2–3 (1923) 3–7.

7. J. Naveh, "Khirbat al-Muqanna–Ekron," *IEJ* 8 (1958) 87–100; 165–70.

8. W. F. Albright in: *The Cambridge Ancient History* (3rd edition; Cambridge: Cambridge University Press [first published as a fascicle, 1966]) vol. 2, part 2, 509 n. 3.

9. Y. Aharoni, "The Northern Boundary of Judah," *PEQ* 90 (1958) 27–31; B. Mazar, "The Cities of the Tribe of Dan," *IEJ* 10 (1960) 66; Z. Kallai, "The Town Lists of Judah, Simeon, Benjamin and Dan," *VT* 8 (1958) 145–46.

10. R. de Vaux, *The Early History of Israel* (Philadelphia: Westminster, 1978) 542; J. A. Emerton, "Some Problems in Genesis XXXVIII," *VT* 25 (1975) 343.

11. On this variation, see Z. Kallai, *The Tribes of Israel: A Study in the Historical Geography of the Bible* (Jerusalem: Bialik Institute, 1967) 171, no. 217 (Hebrew).

12. B. Mazar, "The Cities of the Territory of Dan," *IEJ* 10 (1960) 65–77; Z. Kallai, "Town Lists," 144–48; idem, *The Northern Boundaries of Judah* (Jerusalem: Magnes, 1960) 27–28 (Hebrew); R. de Vaux, *Early History*, 777; N. Na'aman, *Borders and Districts in Biblical Historiography* (Jerusalem: Simor, 1986) 75–118.

13. Z. Kallai, "The Kingdom of Rehoboam," *Eretz-Israel* 10 (1971) 253, map. Several scholars, from A. Alt onward, however, deny the biblical attribution of this list to Rehoboam and suggest a later date for it.

14. B. Mazar, "Campaign of Sennacherib"; N. Na'aman, "Sennacherib's Campaign to Judah and the Date of the *lmlk* Stamps," *VT* 29 (1979) 62–86; idem, "Hezekiah's Fortified Cities and the LMLK Stamps," *BASOR* 261 (1986) 5–21.

2 The Archaeological Expedition to Tel Batash (Timnah)

The Archaeological Expedition to Tel Batash (Timnah) began with three primary objectives:

1. To determine and clarify the stratigraphical and cultural sequence of occupation at Timnah.
2. To provide an academic program in archaeological method and technique, including practical experience on a site of biblical interest.
3. To undertake a regional study in order to clarify the cultural history of the Sorek Valley in the northern Shephelah.

The project was initiated and sponsored for three seasons (1977–79) by New Orleans Baptist Theological Seminary (with additional financial assistance from Mississippi College and Louisiana College) in collaboration with The Hebrew University of Jerusalem. During the nine additional seasons (1981–89), the project and its academic program were sponsored by and directed on behalf of Southwestern Baptist Theological Seminary of Fort Worth, Texas, still in collaboration with The Hebrew University. The expedition was initiated by Expedition Director George L. Kelm, professor of archaeology at Southwestern and directed in collaboration with Archaeological Field Director Amihai Mazar, professor of archaeology at the Institute of Archaeology of The Hebrew University of Jerusalem. A professional and technical staff directed an annual volunteer work force of 30 to 65 students and other volunteers. The expedition is deeply indebted to Linda Kelm for accepting responsibility for correspondence, application evaluation and credit program registration related to volunteer recruitment, as well as for the typing, editing, copying, collating, and binding of field reports following each excavation season.

The initial application for an excavation permit from the Israel Department of Antiquities and Museums envisioned a six-year field project at Tel Batash (Timnah): an initial three-year program (Phase I), followed by a one-year hiatus for research and writing purposes and a reevaluation of our original objectives. Phase II was planned to include an additional three years of excavation and the publication of our final excavation report. The completion of Phase I (1977–1979) was followed by the publication of our first preliminary report. The successes of the first three years and the provision of more adequate funding, following the transition of the Expedition Director from the New Orleans Seminary to the Southwestern Seminary faculty in Fort Worth in 1980, provided the necessary impetus for an extended Phase II of an additional nine years of field work, when a number of innovations and significant administrative guidelines were developed that have influenced the nature of subsequent archaeological field work.

During its twelve seasons of four to six weeks, the expedition contributed to an understanding of the history and cultural development of the biblical town and the surrounding Sorek basin. The results of the excavations have appeared periodically in preliminary reports and more popular articles in archaeological journals.[1] Analysis of the abundant archaeological finds, with the ultimate aim of writing the final technical reports, has been a long and tiring process. Work on the finds from Timnah involved restoring pottery assemblages, drawing finds, cataloging and registering thousands of items, photographing cultural objects, performing laboratory analyses of botanical and faunal remains, writing descriptions of the excavation results, carrying out comparative research on various finds, preparing the plans, sections and other graphic materials for the reports, and preparing

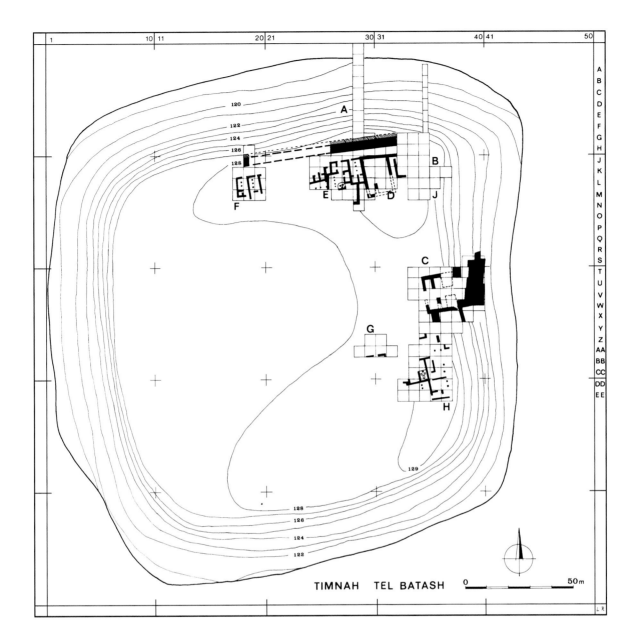

TIMNAH   TEL BATASH

Fig. 2.1. Topographical plan with excavation areas, Tel Batash (Timnah). Architectural remains of Stratum II (7th century B.C.E.) are shown.

computerized analyses of data. A relatively small portion of this work was done at Fort Worth, while the bulk of the work was carried out in the laboratories of the Institute of Archaeology of The Hebrew University of Jerusalem under the supervision of A. Mazar. Responsibility for most of the pottery restoration was shared by Orah Mazar and Linda Kelm, while specialists throughout Israel and the U.S.A. contributed their technical expertise and presented their findings in the final excavation reports that will soon be published. Since 1992, the Philip and Muriel Berman Center of Biblical

Archaeology established at The Hebrew University and the Israel Academy of Sciences have provided major funding for the Timnah research. Mrs. Nava Panitz-Cohen has been responsible for and has supervised many aspects of the research, including the preparation of the loci indexes, pottery plates, and pottery descriptions, while M. Kaplan updated the plans which were initially prepared by L. Ritmeyer, and prepared final inked drawings of the sections. The final excavation reports are scheduled for publication in the *Qedem* series of the Hebrew University. (For a full list of the project's staff, see Appendix B.)

The Stratigraphic Scheme

The stratigraphic sequence at Tel Batash consists of primary and secondary occupational stages. The primary division includes twelve occupational strata identified by Roman numerals. Each stratum represents a city that was destroyed. A further division of most of the strata into occupational subphases was possible, though such subphases were not detected in every sector of each stratum. When observed in several locations, they were identified alphabetically (A, B, etc., with A being the latest phase). These distinctive substrata represent local phases of construction, floor elevations, and various other architectural modifications in each of the main strata, and therefore are not consistent throughout the excavation areas. While a stratum in one sector of the site may have two or more phases, the occupational layer of the same period in another area may exhibit no subphases. The table of the primary strata is presented in Table 2.1.

Areas and Sequence of Excavation

The excavation of Tel Batash gradually expanded along the northern and eastern crests of the mound. Each excavation area was intended to achieve specific objectives in clarifying the historical and cultural sequence of the site's occupation. The topographic plan of the site was divided into a 5 × 5 m grid with alphabetic (north-south) and numerical (west-east) designations. These 5 × 5 m squares were the basic units of excavation in each area.

Table 2.1: Main Strata at Tel Batash (Timnah)

Stratum	Period	Date
I	Persian	
II	Iron Age II	7th century B.C.E.
III	Iron Age II	Destruction, 701 B.C.E. (gap?)
IV	Iron Age II	10th century B.C.E.
V	Iron Age I	Philistine city
VI	Late Bronze IIB	13th–early 12th? centuries B.C.E.
VII	Late Bronze IIA	14th century B.C.E.
VIII	Late Bronze IB	2nd half of 15th century B.C.E.
IX	Late Bronze IA–B	Mid-15th century B.C.E.
X	Late Bronze IA	Mid-16th to early 15th centuries
XI	Middle Bronze IIC	17th–16th centuries B.C.E.
XII	Middle Bronze IIB	18th or 17th centuries B.C.E.
	Chalcolithic	Isolated finds
	Neolithic	Isolated finds

Table 2.2: Seasons and Areas Worked

Years	1977	1978	1979	1981	1982	1983	1984	1985	1986	1987	1988	1989
Seasons	I	II	III	IV	V	VI	VII	VIII	IX	X	XI	XII
Area A	o	o	o									
Area B	o	o	o	o	o	o	o	o	o	o	o	o
Area C	o	o	o	o	o	o	o	o	o		o	o
Area D			o	o			o	o		o		o
Area E				o	o	o	o	o				
Area F						o			o			
Area G						o						
Area H								o	o	o	o	o
Area J										o		

Area A. A step-trench was excavated into the northern slope of the mound (Squares A–H29) during the first three seasons (1977–79). This section, 4 m wide and 40 m long, ran from the crest to the base of the tell and extended below the level of the surrounding alluvial plain. Its excavation was intended to determine the basic stratigraphic sequence of the mound, to expose existing fortifications, and especially to test the hypothesis that a Middle Bronze Age rampart had determined the shape of the mound. These objectives were basically achieved during the first two seasons.

Fig. 2.2. Area A Step-trench on the northern slope of the tell.

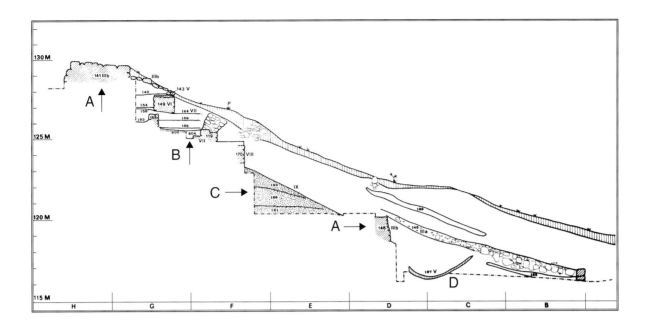

Area B. Excavation in the mound's northeastern quadrant clarified the apparent acropolis of the city, an area 1.0–1.5 m higher than the rest of the mound. This area (located in Squares G–K-33–35), covered 300 sq m (15 × 20 m). Unfortunately, the Iron Age II remains had completely eroded away, and Iron I remains (Stratum V) were discovered directly below topsoil in the southern part of the area. Along the northern crest, even the Iron I materials were eroded and Late Bronze Age remains were found just below topsoil. Since Area B ultimately provided easy access to the second millennium B.C.E. levels at Tel Batash, excavation during all twelve seasons was committed to exposing eight occupation levels (Strata V–XII), covering approximately seven hundred years (eighteenth to eleventh centuries B.C.E.). Exposure of the earlier strata was restricted (as the excavation deepened) by the depth of the excavation. Finally, during the 1989 season, two probes reached virgin soil. Additional study of the Middle Bronze fortifications in the area was made possible in a long trench (excavated by mechanical equipment in 1987) near the mound's northeast corner in Squares A-F-35.

Area C. The Iron II city gates were exposed in a saddle on the eastern crest of the tell. During the first three seasons (1977–79), the stone foundations of the inner gate were

Fig. 2.3. Drawing of section in the slope of the mound (Area A, looking west).
(A) Iron Age II
(B) Late Bronze Age
(C) Middle Bronze Age
(D) Moat

Fig. 2.4. General view of
Area C excavations, 1979.

exposed. In subsequent seasons, the foundations of an impressive outer gate of the Iron Age II city were excavated in
an eastern extension that included the mound's slope. The
excavation ultimately included the limits of the outer and inner Iron Age II gate, an area of 850 sq m. While only the upper two or three strata (into Stratum III) were excavated in
most of this area, more limited excavation during subsequent seasons clarified the building remains and the fortification system from the tenth century and the Iron Age I
(Strata IV–V), and even some Late Bronze Age remains.

Areas D–E. Beginning in the third season, large residential areas of the Iron Age II city were excavated in a
925 sq m area west of Area B (Squares G, H, J, K, L-25–32),
inside the northern city wall. The city wall, an adjoining
street, two buildings of Stratum II, and fragments of additional buildings were exposed. Excavation during subsequent seasons included more restricted areas of Strata III
and IV, while Stratum V was reached in only a few probes.

Area F. (Squares H, J, K, L, M-18–20; total area 150
sq m). Excavation in this isolated area, located 25 m west of
Area E, was restricted to Seasons 6 and 9 and was intended
to expand the exposure of the Stratum II residential quarter.
Two seventh century B.C.E. dwellings were unearthed. The
excavation did not penetrate below Stratum II in this area.

Area G. (Squares Z, AA, BB, CC-29–32; total area 250 sq m). A small area southwest of the Area C gate was examined during the seventh season (1984). Only a few remains of Strata I and II were recovered from the limited exposure.

Area H. (Squares Z, AA, BB, CC, DD, EE-33–37; total area 600 sq m). This large area, adjoining the Area C gate complex on the south, was opened during Season 8 and expanded during Seasons 9–12. The purpose was to examine an elevated area south of the Iron Age II city gate, where presumably public buildings of the Iron Age II city might be found. Private dwellings of Stratum IV, public structures of Stratum III, and an industrial complex of Stratum II were exposed in this area.

Area J. (Squares L, M-34, 35; total area 100 sq m). A southern extension of Area B was opened in 1987 in order to study the Iron Age I period. However, the area was soon abandoned when it became evident that almost all Iron Age remains had been completely eroded. Late Bronze structures were exposed near the surface.

Twelve seasons of excavations during the summers of 1977–79 and 1981–89 exposed the stratigraphic profile of the site, covering all periods from the Middle Bronze II to the Persian period. The results of our excavations, together with excavations carried out at nearby Ekron (Tel Miqne) from 1981 onward, the earlier excavations at Gezer, and the old and renewed excavations at Beth-Shemesh, have provided extensive data for a regional study of the northern Shephelah, which is now one of the most extensively explored regions in Israel.[2]

Excavation Records

Collection and Registration in the Field. Intensive collection of pottery, bones and all other finds was made in the field. Sieving was maintained during the excavation of living surfaces, but otherwise was random and not a continuous practice. Sherds and other finds were collected in baskets numbered in the sequential order allocated to each excavation area.

The Registration Method. The registration of finds at Tel Batash was based on the method widely used in Israeli excavations since the early 1960s, described in detail by Aharoni.[3] This method, however, was improved and adapted for computerization. Since the first season (1977), daily bas-

Fig. 2.6. Excavation in Area D (1989 season).

Top left: Fig. 2.7. Sorting pottery

Above: Fig. 2.8. Sieving excavation debris.

Left: Fig. 2.9. Photographing excavation areas.

ket list forms included coded columns that facilitated processing of the data, first in a dBase II and later in a dBase III Plus program. Each form contained the following columns and codes:

1. Basket number
2. Locus number
3. Height
4. Contents (marked in codes)
5. Stratigraphic layer (marked in codes)
6. Temporary stratum number
7. Nature of the find
8. Nature of the layer to which the basket belongs
9. Pottery sorting
10. Pottery reading
11. Notes

The basket numbers identified the source locations of all finds on the daily graphic representation of the area. These were drawn in 1:100 scale during the early seasons and in

Fig. 2.10. Randy Jones recording elevations with transit.

Fig. 2.11. Architect/Draftsman Leen Ritmeyer sketching gate complex.

1:50 scale during the later seasons. Each basket was assigned to its locus. A locus was defined as a particular stratigraphically homogeneous excavation area, earth layer, wall, or installation. Our numbering system (1977–82) employed a four-digit number for each basket. During later seasons, a new system was introduced in which the letters (A, B, C, etc.) identifying the excavation areas were included in the numbers for both loci and baskets. These letters were followed by one or two digits to identify the number of the season, two additional digits for loci, and three additional digits for baskets. Thus, the first locus number assigned in Area E during the sixth season was E601, and the fifth basket number assigned in Area H during the eleventh season was H11005.

In addition to the daily basket lists, supervisors maintained a daily diary, arranged by loci. The diary described the processes of excavation and any observations made in the field. The work in each locus was summarized on locus sheets that contained all the relevant data on the locus, including its location, definition, upper and lower levels, neighboring loci above and below, a description and drawing of the locus, and lists of baskets and finds from the locus (the latter prepared by the computer program). All the daily basket sheets, loci sheets, and diaries for the areas for each season were typed and bound, with copies kept on file in

Fig. 2.12. Baruch Brandl, Area C supervisor and academic program lecturer.

the Institute of Archaeology of The Hebrew University, Southwestern Baptist Theological Seminary in Fort Worth, Texas, and the archives of the Israel Antiquities Authority.

Fig. 2.13. End-of-the-week volunteer tour of excavation areas.

TIMNAH EXCAVATIONS

Key to Graphic Basket List

Columns 18-19

01 - surface soil

02 - unstratified wash

03 - stratified accumulation

04 - destruction layer

05 - fallen stones

06 - fallen bricks

07 - loose earth

08 - ash layer

09 - accumulation on floor

10 - floor make up

11 - pit

12 - cleaning walls

13 - cleaning sections

14 - foundation trench

15 - balk removal

16 - dismantling walls

17 - robbers' trench

18 - fill

19 - natural soil

20 - cleaning winter debris

21 - oven

22 - gray earth stratified accumulation

23 -

Columns 22-23

01 - sherds

02 - sherds for restoration

03 - complete vessel

04 - bronze

05 - iron

06 - figurine

07 - seal

08 - stone

09 - other small finds

10 - material for analysis

11 - bones

12 - flint

13 -

14 -

15 -

Column 24

1 - sorted, sherds kept

2 - sorted, and cancelled

3 - restoration

4 - wait

Periods
Columns 25-26

1 - Persian

2 - Iron II B-C (9th-7th c.)

  A - 7th cent.
  B - 8th cent.
  C - 9th cent.

3 - Iron II A (10th cent.)

  D - 10th cent.

4 - Iron I

5 - LB

6 - MB

7 - EB

8 - Chalcolithic

9 - mixed

0 - undefined

N - Neolithic

Y - Byzantine

COLOR CODE

Red = Loci numbers
Green = Wall numbers
Black = Baskets & finds
Blue = Special heights
Pencil = Hatching ///

Fig. 2.14. Key to the Graphic Basket List.

SUPERVISOR: COPLAND   06/25/87

```
       |      |      |     |STR|LOC|    |R|      |
BASKET |LOCUS |SQUARE|LEVEL|DEF|STR|CONT|+|PERIOD|          NOTES
-------+------+------+-----+---+---+----+-+------+-----------------------------
D10193|D1035|  L32 | 2970| 03|   | 02|3|      |RELATE TO D10191
D10194|D1036|  L32 | 2940| 03|   | 01|1| 4    |S CTR;6 PAINTED,92 UN-PAI-FLASK?
D10195|D1036|  L32 | 2938| 03|   | 01|1| 4    |N;5 PAINTED,226 UNP,3 BURNISHED
D10196|D1035|  L32 | 2963| 18|   | 09|1|      |BEADS;BALK BURIAL
D10197|D1036|  L32 | 2946| 03|   | 01|1| 45   |SE
D10198|D1035|  L32 | 2963| 18|   | 11|1|      |BONES;BALK BURIAL
D10199|D1033|  M30 | 2937| 01|   | 01|2|      |SURFACE-GENERAL;PIECES TO R?
D10200|D1033|  M30 | 2937| 01|   | 02|3| 2B   |STORE JAR
D10201|D1033|  M30 | 2937| 01|   | 08|1|      |GRIND STONE
D10202|D1036|  L32 | 2940| 03|   | 02|3|      |PILGRIM FLASK
D10203|D1023|  L30 |    0| 13|   | 01|2| 342  |S BALK
D10204|D1023|  L30 | 2915| 13|   | 11|1|      |BONES FROM BURIAL
D10205|D1033|  M30 | 2937| 01|   | 01|3| 2B   |S;POSSIBLE R
D10206|D1033|  M30 | 2950| 01|   | 01|3| 2B   |N; POSSIBLE R
D10207|D1033|  M30 | 2937| 01|   | 09|1|      |LOOM WEIGHT
D10208|D1036|  L32 | 2940| 03|   | 01|1| 4    |12 UNPAINTED;2 PAINTED
D10209|D1036|  L32 | 2938| 03|   | 11|1|      |
D10210|D1035|  L32 | 2941| 03|   | 11|1|      |
D10211|D1035|  L32 | 2941| 03|   | 01|1| 3    |
D10212|D1036|  L32 | 2940| 03|   | 11|1|      |RELATE TO D10194
```

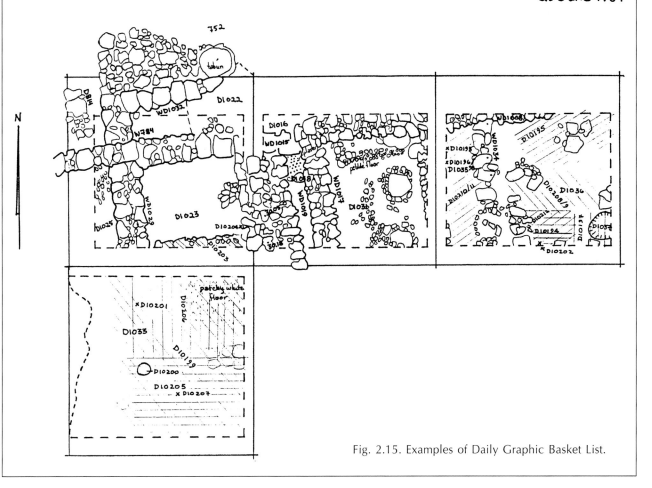

TIMNAH 10
AREA D
25 JUNE 1987

Fig. 2.15. Examples of Daily Graphic Basket List.

TEL BATASH	Season 10 19 87	Area D Square L 32	LOCUS NO. D1007
Date Opened: 16 - 6 - 87 Level: 30.02	Date Closed: 22 - 6 - 87 Level: 29.71	Floor Level: 30.02^E - 29.83^W	Definition: Pebble floor
Loci Above: D1006	Loci Beneath: D1028	Arch. Unit	Combined with: Final Locus:

Borders:

N. balk	S. D1020	E. balk	W. D1020

DESCRIPTION.

Reason for Opening: Pebble - cobble floor appeared under reddish-brown soil

Reason for Closing: Removal of pebble - cobble floor makeup

Data: This pebble floor was preserved only in the NE corner of the square in an area 79 (N-S) × 90 (E-W) cm. next to the northern and eastern balks. The floor was below the level of the Stratum III wall [WD1008] and unfortunately had no relationship with an extant wall. The pottery on the floor was of Stratum IV date. The floor was made up mostly of pebbles but with a few small cobbles up to 30 × 14 cm. in size.

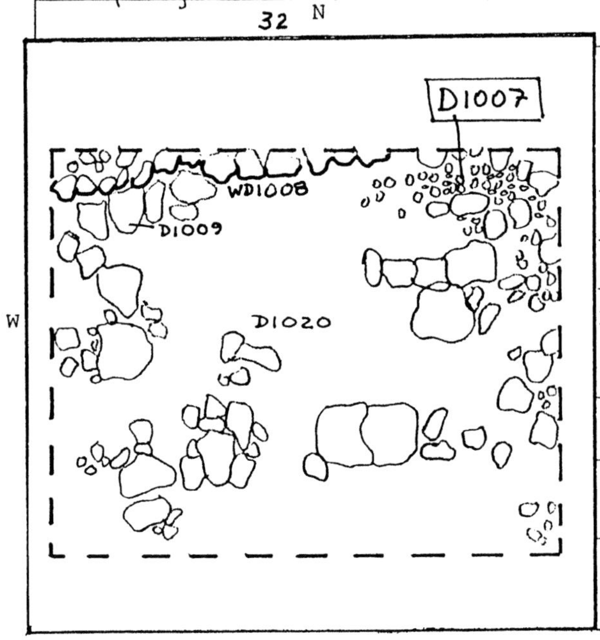

Plans:	Sorted:
Sections:	Restored:
Field Photographs:	Finds Drawings:

Fig. 2.16. Example of a Locus Card.

```
  TEL BATASH        SEASON  10    AREA D        1987               LOCUS    D1007
  BASKET LIST                                                      STRATUM

 |             |      |STR|CON-|R |        |                         |         |
 |BASKET NO.|LEVEL|DEF|TENT|+-|PERIODS|COMMENTS                     |DATE     |
 +----------+-----+---+----+--+-------+--------------------------+---------+
 |  D10031  |3002 | 03| 11 |1 |       |BONES                     |06/16/87|
 |  D10032  |3002 | 03| 01 |1 |   3   |                          |06/16/87|
 |  D10033  |3002 | 03| 08 |1 |       |FLINT                     |06/16/87|
 |  D10034  |3002 | 03| 09 |1 |       |SHELL                     |06/16/87|
 |  D10035  |3002 | 03| 08 |1 |       |SLING STONE               |06/16/87|
 |  D10111  |2983 | 10| 01 |2 |   0   |UNDER PEBBLES             |06/19/87|
 |  D10117  |2971 | 10| 01 |1 |   4   |UNDER COBBLE-PEBBLE FLOOR |06/22/87|
 |  D10118  |2971 | 10| 11 |1 |       |BONES                     |06/22/87|
 +--------------------------------------------------------------------+

 +---SPECIAL FINDS----------------------------------------------------+
 |BASKET No.|      CONTENTS              |  DRAWING  | PHOTOGRAPH      |
 +----------+---------------------------+-----------+-----------------+
 |  D10031  |BONES                      |           |                 |
 |  D10033  |FLINT                      |           |                 |
 |  D10034  |SHELL                      |           |                 |
 |  D10035  |SLING STONE                |           |                 |
 |  D10118  |BONES                      |           |                 |
 |                                                                    |
```

LOCUS DIARY

Area D   L-32   Locus D1007

6.16.87   30.02   This locus consists of a pebble/cobble floor discovered
                           below D1006 in the northeast corner of square L-32.
                           It extends 79 cm S of the N balk and 90 cm W of the E
                           balk. Its cobbles range in size from 30 X 14 cm to
                           20 X 20 cm. Above it was found a concentration of
              29.98   pottery (basket D10021).
                           It does not appear to be related to any walls or
                           architectural features at this time. It is clearly below
                           the Stratum III wall WD1008 however.

6.17.86   Cleaning continued to the south and west to see if this
                           floor continued. The cobble-pebble floor did not extend
              29.83   farther than the limits described above.

6.19.87   Pebble floor removed. Below it was compact gray brown
              29.73 LL   soil. Locus closed. New locus D1028.

Fig. 2.17. Sample of Basket List (sorted by loci) and Locus Diary.

Endnotes

1. The following preliminary reports were published on the excavations: G. L. Kelm and A. Mazar, "Three Seasons of Excavations at Tel Batash—Biblical Timnah," *BASOR* 248 (1982) 1–36; idem, "Tel Batash (Timnah) Excavations: Second Preliminary Report (1981–1982)," *BASOR Supplement* 23 (1985) 108–16; idem, "Excavations at Tel Batash (Timnah), 1984–1988 (Third Preliminary Report)," *BASOR Supplement* 27 (1990) 47–67; idem, "Excavating in Samson Country," *BAR* 15/1 (1989) 36–49; idem, "Batash, Tel (Timnah)," in *The New Encyclopedia of Archaeological Excavations in the Holy Land* (rev. ed.; ed. E. Stern; Jerusalem and New York, 1993) 152–57.

Annual reports were published in Notes and News, *IEJ*: 27 (1977) 167–68; 29 (1979) 195–96; 29 (1979) 241–43; 32 (1982) 153–54; 33 (1983) 126; 33 (1983) 269–71; 35 (1985) 200–201; 36 (1986) 107–9; 39 (1989) 108–10.

2. See the articles on Gezer, Beth-Shemesh, and Tel Miqne (Ekron) in E. Stern (ed.), *New Encyclopedia of Archaeological Excavations*; S. Gitin, "Tel Miqne-Ekron: A Type Site for the Inner Coastal Plain in the Iron Age II Period," in *Recent Excavations in Israel: Studies in Iron Age Archaeology* (AASOR 49; ed. S. Gitin and W. G. Dever; 1989) 23–58; T. Dothan, "The Arrival of the Sea Peoples: Cultural Diversity in Early Iron Age Canaan," in ibid., 1–14; A. Mazar, "The Northern Shephelah in the Iron Age: Some Issues in Biblical History and Archaeology," in *Scripture and Other Artifacts: Essays in Honor of Philip J. King* (ed. M. D. Coogan, J. C. Exum, and L. E. Stager; Louisville, 1994) 247–67.

3. Y. Aharoni, *Beer-sheba I: Excavations at Tel Beer-sheba 1969–1971 Seasons* (Tel Aviv, 1973) 119–32.

3 From the Neolithic to the Middle Bronze Age: The Foundation of Tel Batash

The Sorek Valley During the Seventh to Third Millennia B.C.E.

Excellent environmental and climatic conditions in the northern Shephelah attracted early settlement to the region. A Pre-Pottery Neolithic site, probably dating from the seventh millennium B.C.E., was discovered by T. Kaminer, a member of Kibbutz Zorah, just 500 m northwest of Tel Batash along the Sorek's southern bank. Though the site has not been excavated scientifically, the numerous stone pestles and mortars discovered there provide evidence of extensive grain agriculture carried on by the valley's earliest settlers. Another Pre-Pottery Neolithic A site in the region, Hatula, lies south of the Latrun monastery.[1] Such evidence suggests that the Sorek Valley was inhabited during this dramatic period when the first farming communities were established at such sites as Jericho and ᶜAin Ghazal. These Neolithic settlements flourished in the conditions of the northern Shephelah, conditions that were ideally suited to the emergence of the revolutionary sedentary economies characteristic of the Neolithic period.

The Pottery-Neolithic period (late sixth–early fifth millennia B.C.E.) is represented in this region at the site of Teluliot

Batash (Arabic *Tuleilat Batashi*), just a short distance east of Timnah on the northern bank of the Sorek. There J. Kaplan excavated the remains of a village from this period that yielded some of the earliest pottery ever found in Palestine.[2] Some Neolithic and Chalcolithic pottery sherds found at Tel Batash (mainly in the fill of the Middle Bronze earthen rampart) suggest that a small settlement, similar to that of Teluliot Batashi, probably was destroyed during the Middle Bronze earth-moving operation that created Timnah's defensive rampart. During the Chalcolithic period, the rich alluvial soils of the valley attracted even more significant settlement, as indicated by two Ghassulian Chalcolithic sites discovered farther east along the Sorek Valley.

During the final centuries of the fourth millennium B.C.E., a proliferation of unfortified villages appeared in the entire country, as a result of the expansion of the Chalcolithic agrarian society and perhaps the arrival of new peoples in the country. This period, known as the Early Bronze Age I, is represented in the Sorek Valley by two sites excavated north and south of the modern town of Beth-Shemesh. At Hartuv, one of these sites, A. Mazar and P. de Miroschedji uncovered a unique architectural complex with a line of standing stones, possibly the remains of a sanctuary. The other site is Horvat ᶜIllin, south of Beth-Shemesh, where a village was excavated by E. Braun for the Israel Antiquities Authority.[3]

At the beginning of the third millennium B.C.E., these Early Bronze I villages consolidated into large, strongly fortified cities during an intensive process of urbanization that followed throughout the country (Early Bronze Age II–III). No such city developed in the Sorek basin, but Gezer to the north and Yarmut to the south (the largest Early Bronze city in the Shephelah) became important Early Bronze urban centers and shared or vied for control of the Sorek basin.

The collapse of Canaan's thriving Early Bronze city-state culture (ca. 2400–2300 B.C.E.) was followed by a sparse population of farmers and seminomadic pastoralists during the next two to three centuries. Major urban sites of the previous period were abandoned completely or resettled with unfortified villages of poorly constructed "hovels." An entirely new settlement pattern emerged throughout the country. At Jebel Qaaqir, in the southern Shephelah west of

Hebron, the remains of cave dwellings, poor huts, and a large cemetery nearby are characteristic of this Early–Middle Bronze Age transitional period. No remains of this "Intermediate Bronze Age," however, have been found thus far in the Sorek region.

The Middle Bronze Age

Historical Setting. The first half of the second millennium B.C.E. saw the return of vigorous urban life to the Levant. The establishment of the Canaanite culture throughout the country and the founding of cities and towns such as Timnah must be seen against the background of broader historical developments throughout the Near East.[4] The West Semitic peoples of the Levant, after establishing city-state dynasties, gradually expanded into both Mesopotamia and Lower Egypt and established local dynasties there as well. During the eighteenth–seventeenth centuries B.C.E., vital international diplomatic and commercial relations extended from Egypt to the headwaters of the Persian Gulf.

The first part of this era, the Middle Bronze IIA period (called by some archaeologists Middle Bronze I, ca. 2000–1800/1750 B.C.E.), is contemporary with the Middle Kingdom in Egypt. A gradual revival of urban life was characterized by new techniques and forms of pottery vessels, metallurgy, architecture, burial customs, and so forth. Urban and rural settlements were founded mainly along the coastal plain of Palestine. Some of the cities, such as Kabri, Akko, Tel Burgah, Tel Mevorakh, Tel Zeror, Tel Hefer, Tel Poleg, and Aphek, were fortified with massive walls, and some of them were surrounded by earthen ramparts. Settlement south of the Yarkon appears to have been less extensive or at least slower in its development and more rural in character. One exception was the coastal site of Yavneh Yam, due west of Timnah, which was surrounded by a huge square earthen rampart and may have been founded during this period.[5] In the southern Shephelah's interior, Tell Beit Mirsim also emerged as a small town during the Middle Bronze IIA.

While Egypt suffered a period of decline during the Second Intermediate Period, the Canaanite culture of Palestine–Syria with its local city-states experienced unusual prosperity. This period (18–16th centuries B.C.E.) was a time of

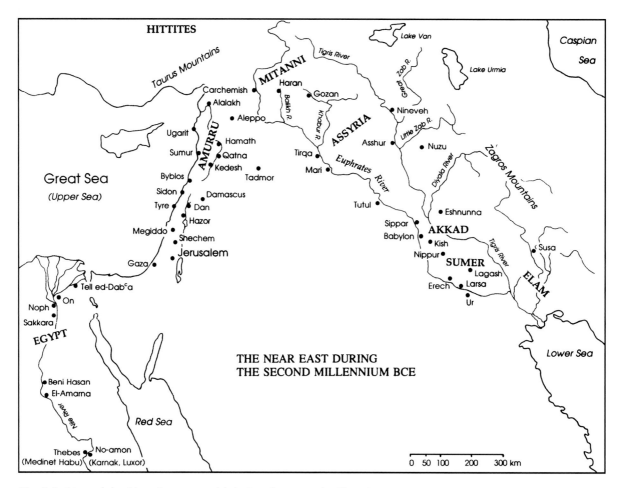

Fig. 3.1. Map of the Near Eastern world during the second millennium B.C.E.

great urban expansion in Canaan. Many cities grew and were fortified by massive earth works. The strength of the Canaanites finds expression in their seizure of the eastern Delta of Egypt, where they established the local "Hyksos" rule (the Fifteenth Dynasty). The capital of the Hyksos was at Avaris, biblical Zoan (modern Tell el-Dabᶜa), which according to the biblical tradition was founded seven years after the founding of Hebron (Num 13:22). The indigenous Canaanite West-Semitic population was now intermingled with a new ethnic element—the Hurrians (biblical Horites), who arrived from northern Mesopotamia. Hurrian names have been found on a few documents from this period, including one from Gezer, north of Tel Batash.

Tel Batash during the Middle Bronze Age
(Strata XII-XI)

The Middle Bronze Age in the Shephelah. In the Shephelah, urban development did not get under way until quite late in the Middle Bronze Age II, mostly after 1800 B.C.E.. However, from the eighteenth century onward the process of urbanization was rapid and impressive. Tel Batash was founded as one of a chain of fortified cities in the region. Gezer, 8 km to the north, was well fortified with a glacis, city wall and monumental towers.[6] Tel Miqne, just 6 km to the west, was a large 45 acre site, founded in the Middle Bronze Age and probably surrounded by earth ramparts (as yet unexcavated). Beth-Shemesh, about 7 km to the southeast, was also characterized by a strategic location along the Sorek River. Other cities existed in the southern Shephelah, such as Lachish and Tell Beit Mirsim. We assume that Tel Batash was a secondary town within the territory of either Gezer or Tel Miqne.

The foundation of Tel Batash in this period can be seen as part of the contemporary growth of population and intensification of urbanization. The site became an important fortified town, enjoying the economic and strategic advantages of the fertile Sorek Valley. The superb environmental conditions assured its continuous occupation during the next thirteen or fourteen centuries. The new fortified town thrived as a result of its rich agricultural setting and its control of commercial traffic along a major route through the Sorek Valley, linking the Via Maris in the coastal plain to the west with the inner Shephelah's north-south road along the base of the hills near Beth-Shemesh, and with the heart of the central hill country to the east.

The Earthen Rampart. The physical appearance of Tel Batash, with its square shape, its orientation to the points of the compass, and its concave upper surface led us to suspect the existence of a Middle Bronze Age defensive rampart even before the excavations began. Excavation of a step-trench into the northern slope of the mound (Area A) was begun in the first season (1977) to clarify the nature of the town's defenses. This trench, 4 m wide and 40 m long, provided our first glimpse of the mound's archaeological profile. It proved that the Canaanite city was indeed founded in the Middle Bronze Age II and was surrounded by earthen ramparts.

In the step-trench, below a stratum containing pure Late Bronze pottery, a small section of the Middle Bronze Age rampart was exposed; it consisted of layers of reddish-brown alluvial soil mixed with large quantities of pebbles taken from the Sorek riverbed. Traces of white lime suggested that the surface of the massive rampart, which had a gradient of 25 degrees, had been protected by a plaster finish.

At the base of the mound, excavation in the trench to a depth of approximately two meters below the present level of the surrounding plain exposed the presence of a wide moat that had surrounded the Middle Bronze city. The moat and the rampart were presumably constructed contemporaneously as integral parts of a comprehensive defensive system.

A second trench on the northern slope, located 25 m to the east, was excavated near the northeastern corner of the mound (as a continuation of Area B). Here the trench extended north of a massive Middle Bronze citadel located in the corner of the mound. The excavation of the rampart was started in the usual way. When the continuation of manual labor was deemed impractical, conferring little or no scientific advantage, the work was continued with mechanical equipment. The result was a 2.8-m trench extending 25 m from the level of the plain directly to the base of the northern citadel's wall. This trench provided clear insight into the

Fig. 3.2. Section through the Middle Bronze rampart and fortifications near northeastern corner of the mound (Area B, looking east). Note penetration of Iron Age II revetment wall (B925).

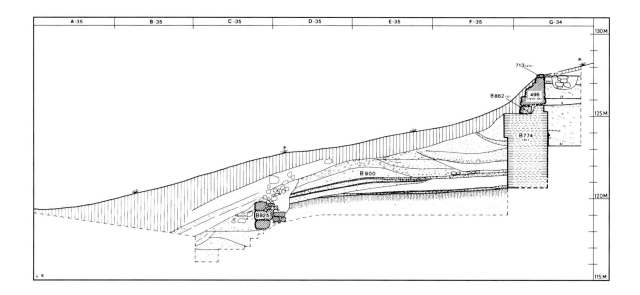

nature of the rampart's construction, from virgin soil to the present topsoil.

Founded on the level alluvial plain near the Sorek's southern bank, the rampart, near the northeast corner of the mound, was preserved to a height of 4.5 m and was at least 25 m long. Courses of brook pebbles in the lowest levels of the northern extension of the trench suggested that an earlier course of the Sorek may have been nearer the town site than it is today. The thin, consecutive layers of clay and pure sand forming the lowest layer of the rampart may have been intended to ensure proper drainage. Most of the rampart consisted of alternating, partly integrated layers of brown alluvial soil and pebbles. These sequential layers of earth and pebbles were bonded and anchored together to reduce erosion and to enhance the rampart's structural strength. The inner (southern) side of the rampart approached and was supported by a massive mudbrick wall, part of the citadel in the northeastern corner of the mound. Both rampart and wall had originally been much higher. The high citadel wall had so dominated the rampart that archers on the citadel's parapet could effectively defend against enemy attempts at scaling the rampart. Unfortunately, over twenty-five hundred years of erosion along the slope has precluded any estimate of the original height of the rampart's crest, the angle of its original slope and the height of the wall above it.

The earthen ramparts surrounding all four sides of the mound created a formidable defensive perimeter for the town. The interior part of the town lay below the level of these ramparts. Though more than one thousand years of continuous occupation and the regular destruction and rebuilding of the town have tended to fill the huge crater created by the ramparts, the surface of the mound remains slightly concave even today. All occupational strata in the town slant toward the center of the mound as a natural consequence of construction against the inner slope of the rampart. The occupational strata of the Middle Bronze Age within the perimeter of the earthen ramparts were buried beneath thick accumulations of later occupation debris. Unfortunately they were reached only in a very limited area during the last three seasons of excavations.

The sophistication of the massive fortification construction at Timnah is consistent with architectural features

Fig. 3.3. Aerial view of Tel Batash, showing the geometric shape created by its Middle Bronze Age ramparts.

uncovered at other Middle Bronze Age urban sites throughout the Levant. The location of some of these towns on level alluvial plains required massive solid fortification systems. The earthen ramparts were invented to elevate the vertical defensive walls and reduce their vulnerability to tunneling and the use of battering rams and other siege techniques. Timnah, with its massive earthworks, apparently was only one of the smaller links in a chain of cities throughout the country that were surrounded by such earthen ramparts (Dan, Hazor, Kabri, Tel Mevorakh, Tel Burgah, Shechem, Yavneh-Yam, Tel Miqne(?), Tel Masos); similar towns are known from Syria (Carchemish, Tell Mardikh/Ebla, and Qatna).[7] The ramparts of these sites may have reached heights of 10–15 m above the surrounding plain.

The square plan of the Tel Batash ramparts is paralleled at Yavneh-Yam, northwest of Tel Batash, and at Qatna in Syria (where the rampart is 1 km square).[8] The ramparts of Qatna, as at Timnah, are oriented exactly to the points of the compass. A similar, though much smaller, square fortification (with sides of 375 m) was discovered at Tell Sefinet-Nebi-Nouh in Syria. Right angles and rectangular plans in the design of such ramparts also are known at Hazor, Dan, and Tel Masos.[9] Rampart construction in square or rectangular shapes was thus not an uncommon practice during the Middle Bronze Age, and Timnah has provided one of the best examples of this defensive plan.

The artificial rampart was only one, though the most prominent, feature of the Middle Bronze Age urban fortification system. The other type was the earthen *glacis*, which is found at sites with pre-existing slopes. Such fortification systems have been discovered at Jericho, Akko, Shiloh, Ashkelon, and other sites. In both types, enormous quantities of earth and other building materials had to be moved to the site, sometimes from distant sources. The logistics of such construction must have required sophisticated organization of a type that could only be initiated and maintained by a centralized authority. The Middle Bronze fortification systems thus serve as evidence for the vitality and stability of the king's jurisdiction in the city-states scattered throughout the entire region of Syria-Palestine. They also provide evidence of the need for strong fortifications in a region fragmented by many rival petty states.

Fig. 3.4. Middle Bronze IIB–C scarabs.

The Middle Bronze Age Citadel in Area B

A massive citadel, dated to the Middle Bronze Age and located in the northeastern corner of the mound, was partially excavated in Area B. Removal of a floor of the earliest Late Bronze level (Stratum X) toward the end of the 1983 season first exposed the massive mudbrick walls belonging to this citadel. Its outer (northern and eastern) walls were located at the very edge of the mound. They were plastered with clay on their inner faces and preserved to a maximum height of 4.5 m (at least 36–40 mudbrick courses). The northern wall, 2.7 m thick, formed the inner face of the earthen rampart. The eastern wall is very massive, though its exact width is unknown. On the west, there is a 3.35-m-wide mudbrick wall which must have been an inner wall in the citadel. Two large square rooms were excavated in the area of this citadel, but they probably comprise only a small part of this

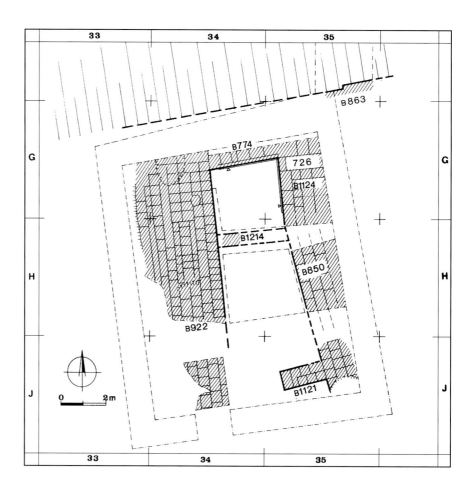

Fig. 3.5. Plan of Stratum XI Middle Bronze IIB citadel in Area B.

large and massive structure. More than two meters of fallen mudbrick debris was found in these rooms; beneath this was a 0.2-m-thick layer of burnt wood and black ash on the floors, which contained a few pottery sherds from the final phase of the Middle Bronze Age II, ca. 1600 B.C.E. (Stratum XI). This floor sealed a thick fill covering an earlier floor (Stratum XII). The earlier floor yielded a few pottery sherds from an earlier phase of the Middle Bronze Age II, perhaps of the eighteenth century B.C.E. This floor is the only evidence that points to the foundation of the citadel, and perhaps of the entire fortification system, in the eighteenth century B.C.E. We did not find any clear evidence of a Middle Bronze settlement before the establishment of the fortifications. However, it is important to note that excavation of the earliest occupational stratum was very limited.

The limitations of the excavation have precluded any clarification of the entire defensive system beyond the cita-

Fig. 3.6. Probes into Middle Bronze strata within the outer stone walls of Late Bronze patrician house in Area B (looking northwest).

Fig. 3.7. Mudbrick walls of MB IIB citadel below northern stone wall of Late Bronze patrician house in Area B.

del complex in the northeastern corner of the mound. It is possible that only the strategic corners of the town's fortifications were reinforced with citadels, while the central span of each of the town's four walls was sustained by the rampart's inner slopes, possibly with an interior wall and occasional towers that have not been preserved.

Endnotes

1. See "Hatula-, Hurvat," in *The New Encyclopedia of Archaeological Excavations in the Holy Land* (rev. ed.; ed. E. Stern; Jerusalem and New York, 1993) 588–99.

2. J. Kaplan, "Excavations at Teluliot Batashi in the Vale of Sorek," *Eretz-Israel* 5 (1958) 9–24 (Hebrew).

3. On Hartuv, see A. Mazar and P. de Miroschedji, "Hartuv, 1985," *IEJ* 36 (1986) 109.

4. W. G. Dever, "The Beginning of the Middle Bronze Age in Syria-Palestine," in *Magnalia Dei—The Mighty Acts of God: Essays on the Bible and Archaeology in Memory of G. Ernest Wright* (ed. F. M. Cross, W. E. Lemke, and P. D. Miller; Garden City, N.Y.: Doubleday, 1976) 3–38; A. Mazar, *Archaeology of the Land of the Bible, 10,000–586 B.C.E.* (New York: Doubleday, 1990) 192; A. Kempinski, "The Middle Bronze Age," in *The Archaeology of Ancient Israel* (ed. A. Ben-Tor; New Haven: Yale University Press, 1992) 159–210.

5 J. Kaplan, Yavneh Yam. In *Encyclopedia of Archaeological Excavations in the Holy Land*, Vol. IV. (eds.) M. Avi-Yonah and E. Stern. Jerusalem: Massada 1978: 1216–1217.

6. J.D. Seger, "The MB II Fortifications at Shechem and Gezer: A Hyksos Retrospective," *Eretz-Israel* 12 (1975) 34*–35*.

7. J. Kaplan, "Further Aspects of the Middle Bronze II Fortifications in Palestine," *ZDPV* 91 (1975) 1–17; P. Parr, "The Origin of the Rampart Fortifications of the Middle Bronze Age in Palestine and Syria," *ZDPV* 84 (1968) 18–45; P. Marrasini, "Sui 'Camp fortificati' nell'eta di Mari," *Oriens Antiquus* 10 (1971) 107–22; A. Kempinski, "Middle and Late Bronze Age Fortifications," in *The Architecture of Ancient Israel* (ed. A. Kempinski and R. Reich; Jerusalem, 1992) 127–42; I. Finkelstein, "Middle Bronze 'Fortifications': A Reflection of Social Organization and Political Formations," *Tel Aviv* 19 (1992) 201–20.

8. Le Comte [R.] du Mesnil du Buisson, "Les Ruines d'el-Mishrife au Nord-Est de Homs," *Syria* 7 (1926) 292–93.

9. Y. Yadin, *Hazor, the Head of All Those Kingdoms* (The Schweich Lectures of the British Academy, 1970; London: Oxford University, 1972) 15–17, fig. 3; A. Biran, *Biblical Dan* (Jerusalem, 1994) 59–74; Y. Aharoni, V. Fritz, and A. Kempinski, "Excavations at Tel Masos, Preliminary Report on the First Season, 1972," *Tel Aviv* 1 (1974) 65, fig. 1.

4 Tel Batash in the Late Bronze Age

Historical Setting

The political and socio-economic equilibrium between the West Semitic city-states of the Levant in the Middle Bronze Age came to an end in the middle of the second millennium B.C.E. The most significant impact on the southern Levant was the Egyptian expulsion of its foreign rulers (the "Hyksos") and Egypt's subsequent military efforts to establish control over the trade routes and economic resources of Canaan. In northern Syria, Hittite raids at the end of the seventeenth century B.C.E. brought an end to the kingdom of Yamhad with its capital at Aleppo, one of the most prosperous kingdoms of the Middle Bronze Age. Vital lines of communication and trade were disrupted. The Hurrians in northern Mesopotamia and northern Syria established the kingdom of Mitanni. Some of them filtered southward into Palestine, where they added a non-Semitic element to the local population.

Beginning in the mid-sixteenth century B.C.E., military campaigns by successive Egyptian pharaohs of the newly-established Eighteenth Dynasty brought havoc and destruction to numerous Middle Bronze Age cities, especially in southern Canaan.[1] Following the three-year siege and ultimate capture of Sharuhen (Tell el-ᶜAjjul?),[2] other sites in the

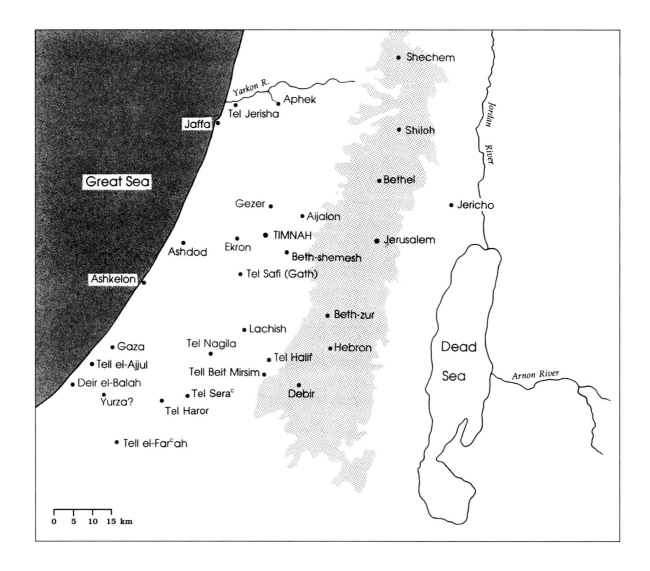

Fig. 4.1. Map of southern Canaan during the Late Bronze Age, ca. 1550–1200 B.C.E.

Negev, including Tell el-Far°ah(S), Tel Malhata and Tel Masos, were destroyed. In the coastal plain and Shephelah, Timnah,[3] Tel Miqne, Yavneh Yam, Gezer, and Aphek were laid waste at the end of the Middle Bronze Age. The cultural disruption was widespread. Major cities and many villages in the northern coastal region (Kabri), in the central hill country (Hebron, Beth Zur, Jerusalem, and Shiloh) and even in the Jordan Valley (Jericho) were destroyed or abandoned. However, some of these cities soon revived, and the disrupted urban Canaanite culture was generally restored. Major cities, such as Hazor, Megiddo, and Beth Shean in the north, were not damaged and continued to thrive in the Late Bronze Age. The continuity of Canaanite culture was maintained and some of the earlier vitality was regained in spite of the disruptive and punitive nature of periodic Egyptian military incursions.[4]

Early in Egypt's New Kingdom period, the most important pharaoh of the Eighteenth Dynasty, Thutmosis III (ca. 1490–1436 B.C.E.) consolidated Egyptian control over Canaan. This he achieved first by his victory at Megiddo over an extensive Canaanite confederacy and later with a series of at least sixteen punitive expeditions. During the fifteenth century Egypt's major enemy was Mitanni, the Hurrian kingdom dominating the northern portions of Syria and Mesopotamia. Vigilance along the northern frontier bordering the Hurrian realm during the reign of Amenophis II, Thutmosis III's successor, and control of the "Via Maris" (the primary international trade route linking Egypt and Syria), demanded excessive exploitation of Canaan's natural resources. Though the primary objectives of the Eighteenth Dynasty pharaohs included control of the major trade routes with Mesopotamia and the maintenance of an extensive buffer zone between the Nile Delta and real or imagined enemies in the northeast, the direct effect of this policy in Canaan was the immense burden of supplying Egypt's military adventures in the Levant and an ever-expanding exploitation of Canaan's population and agrarian surplus by levied tribute.[5] Any Canaanite reticence in meeting Egyptian needs or demands in fostering commercial and military objectives, especially by towns and localities in the immediate vicinity of their primary routes, was doubtless met with an immediate retaliatory response. Raw materials like timber and copper were exploited by the Egyptians in Canaan. Egyptian government was achieved by establishing Egyptian troops and administrators at several strongholds like Gaza and Beth Shean. The local rulers of Canaanite cities retained their autonomy but were loyal vassals of the Egyptian empire.

The most important historical source for this period is the archive found at the capital of Akhenaten (Amenophis IV) at el-Amarna, which provides insight into life in Canaan during the fourteenth century B.C.E. Despite the complaints of local princes concerning an Egyptian military presence too weak to maintain peaceful coexistence among rival urban centers, the Amarna correspondence mentions several Egyptian regional administrative centers. These cities were supposedly committed to the collection of taxes and tribute,

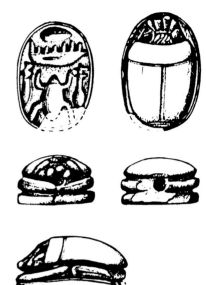

Fig. 4.2. Late Bronze Age scarab of Thutmosis III.

the surveillance and maintenance of the road systems, the equipping and provision of military personnel and the administration of forced labor. Administered by regional Egyptian or Egyptian-trained commissioners, such centers with their small military contingents (archers or chariots) sustained an effective Egyptian domination. Tribute from royal lands, such as the Jezreel and parts of the coastal plain (Sharon and Philistia) and the extortion of staple foodstuffs from smaller settlements surrounding Egyptian administrative centers depleted local economies and significantly contributed to the decline of Canaan during the Late Bronze Age.

During this period, the *Habiru*, a non-citizen element with no land, were identified with both productive activity (often servile, menial work, or as mercenaries) and with destructive occupations (banditry) in their apparent attempts to find a place in the established economic and social framework.

The Late Bronze Canaanite Town at Tel Batash

The Late Bronze Age at Tel Batash yielded a sequence of five strata, reflecting extensive and dramatic destruction and rebuilding during a comparatively short period in the fifteenth-thirteenth centuries B.C.E. During this time, Tel Batash seems to have been a small Canaanite town in the territory of Gezer, the main city-state in the region. Gezer is located on a prominent ridge overlooking both the Valley of Aijalon to the east and the coastal plain with the Via Maris to the west. The el-Amarna archive of the fourteenth century B.C.E. included several letters written by Gezer's king Milkilu to the pharaohs Amenophis III and IV. Gezer appears in these letters as an autonomous city-state, ruling an extensive area in the northern Shephelah. Timnah, though probably part of the territory of Gezer, was vulnerable to attacks, perhaps by *Habiru* and other local enemies. The small and undefended town suffered severe destruction every half century or so, while Gezer remained intact. Timnah's strategic central location within the Sorek's productive alluvial plain and control of a major route into the central hill country probably contributed to the regular attacks and the vulnerability reflected in the successive destruction levels.

Primary study of Timnah's Late Bronze strata was limited to the northeastern quadrant of the mound, with a step-trench section (Area A) cut into the northern slope and an extensive exposure of Late Bronze occupational strata on the highest point of the mound (Area B). A series of architectural units excavated here proved to be among the most interesting and rewarding found, though the exposed areas were too limited to deduce a general town plan from them. The town clearly lacked a defensive wall, and the outer walls of adjoining houses apparently formed a defensive perimeter. Towns without city walls are characteristic of this period, a phenomenon that reflects the political conditions of Canaanite cities under restrictive Egyptian rule.

Fig. 4.3. General view of patrician houses in Area B (looking north, at end of 1988 season).

The First Late Bronze Town (Stratum X)

Only limited exposure of the first Late Bronze town was achieved. Robbers' trenches outlined the limits of a room with an excellent floor, partly plastered and partly paved with plastered cobblestones. Building materials from the large structure to which this room belonged had apparently

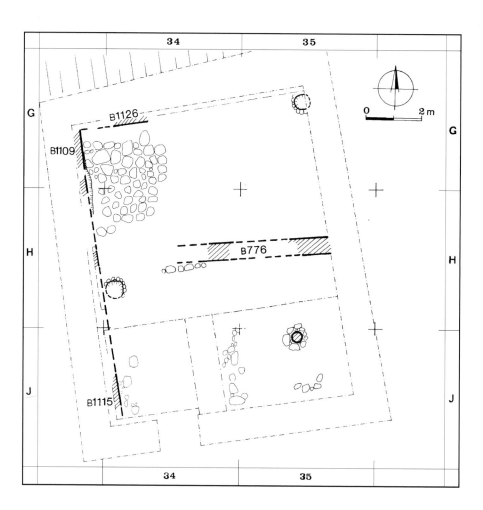

Fig. 4.4. Plan of building remains of Stratum X (Middle Bronze II–Late Bronze I transition) in Area B.

been reused in the subsequent Stratum IX building. The thick layer (0.8 m) of burnt brick, ash, and other destruction debris on the Stratum X floor provided vivid evidence of its fiery end.

Restorable pottery on the Stratum X floors mainly consisted of unpainted local ware typical of the end of the Middle Bronze Age and the beginning of the Late Bronze Age. Two large storage jars (*pithoi*) were characteristic of the period. Among the few diagnostic sherds found, one of bichrome ware and a few imported Cypriot sherds including monochrome and Cypriot white-slip ware suggest commercial connections with Cyprus, probably at the end of the sixteenth century B.C.E. Such trade connections would have predated Egypt's hegemony over Canaan.

The remains of the Stratum X house, though limited, represent the first evidence of elaborate Late Bronze dwellings, probably belonging to upper-class residents who main-

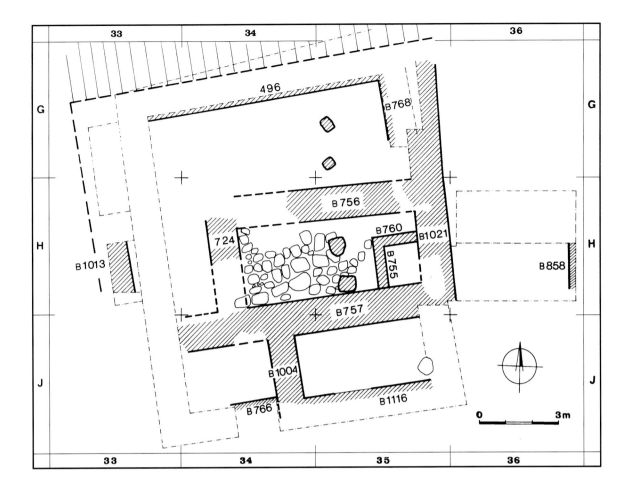

Fig. 4.5. Plan of Stratum IXA building remains in Area B.

tained continuity throughout the sequence of prosperity and disaster.

Canaanite Timnah Rebuilt (Stratum IX)

The Stratum IX building, constructed on the destruction debris of its predecessor, had massive stone walls (1.25 m wide) and measured at least 13 × 13 m. Four pillar bases of flat stones in its eastern part supported the roof or a second story. Various architectural changes and partition walls appeared to belong to later structural modifications.

A second episode of destruction is reflected by an accumulation of charcoal and burnt bricks (0.8 m thick) on its beaten earth floor. The local and imported Cypriot pottery found here was dated to the fifteenth century B.C.E., after the conquests of Thutmosis III. The corpus of restorable pottery recovered from the floor facilitated a refinement of the typological development of the contemporary local pottery.

Canaanite Timnah Rebuilt a Third Time (Stratum VIII)

The new patrician house (Building 471), constructed on the ruins of the Stratum IX building, was almost completely exposed. This 13.3 × 13.6 m building (180 sq m) is one of the finest examples of Late Bronze domestic architecture yet excavated. The northern, eastern, and southern walls of the previous building served as foundations for the new building. Its outer walls were massive (1.00–1.15 m wide), constructed of two lines of large stones. The building's only entrance was from a courtyard on the south. Immediately inside the entrance, a wooden staircase in a narrow corridor on the right provided access to the second story. The ground floor was divided into a large hall on the east and two square rooms on the west. The hall (4.6 × 8.6 m; over 40 sq m) had a well-preserved cobblestone floor and a row of five protruding stone slabs that had served as bases for wooden pillars supporting the ceiling and the upper floor. Burnt brick debris (0.7 m thick) with large concentrations of burnt wood—probably remains of the collapsed second story superstructure—covered the floor of the hall. The two rooms (2.80 × 3.15 and 2.30 × 3.00 m) had plastered floors and entrances in their northeastern corners. The building's western wing had a series of four narrow cells or enclosures that appeared to lack openings. Presumably these small rooms, if used for storage, could only be entered at a level above the heights of their preserved walls.

This large building, without close Canaanite parallels to its extraordinary plan, probably served as a patrician house. Like its predecessors, it was destroyed in a fierce conflagration. Burnt brick debris, charcoal, and ash filled all the areas sealed by the cobblestone floor of the following Stratum VII building. An extensive collection of pottery vessels was recovered from various rooms, with one room yielding layers of broken storage jars and other vessels. A challenging restoration process clarified vessel distribution in the rooms of Building 471 as categorized in Table 4.1.

Table 4.1. Distribution of Vessels in Rooms of Building 471

Contents	475	492	467	494	Total
Bowls	5	8	11	2	26
Kraters	–	3	–	–	3
Chalices	–	1	–	–	1
Cooking pots	4	2	14	–	20
Storage jars	4	14	19	4	41*
Jugs	4	6	9	3	22
Juglets	1	1	2	–	4
Varia	3	1	2	–	6
Total	21	36	57	9	123

*Seven are painted.

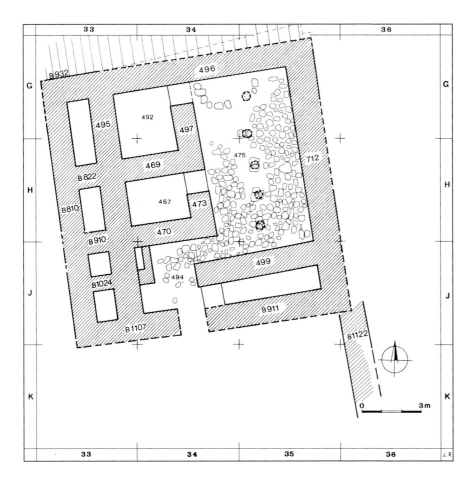

Fig. 4.6. Plan of Stratum VIII Building in Area B (15th century B.C.E.).

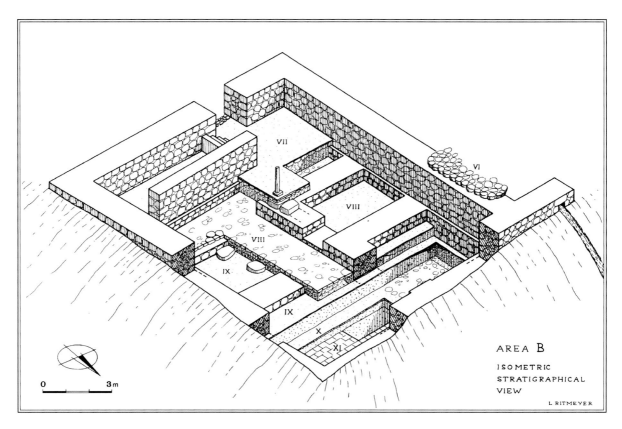

Fig. 4.7. Isometric view of Late Bronze Age strata in Area B (looking southwest).

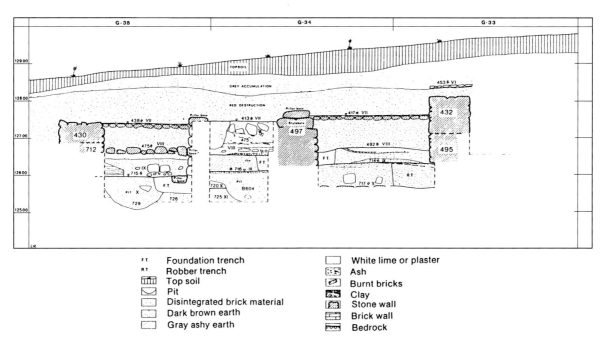

F T	Foundation trench		White lime or plaster
R T	Robber trench		Ash
	Top soil		Burnt bricks
	Pit		Clay
	Disintegrated brick material		Stone wall
	Dark brown earth		Brick wall
	Gray ashy earth		Bedrock

Fig. 4.8. Stratigraphic section through Late Bronze layers in the northern part of Area B (view to south).

With only a few sherds of imported Cypriot (Base-Ring II) pottery and no Mycenaean imports, the pottery consisted primarily of local shapes that were almost indistinguishable from those found in the subsequent Stratum VII. The most prominent shape is a group of large jars with four handles and a small collar-ridge at the base of the neck. One storage jar was uniquely decorated with a black-and-red painting of a procession of human and animal figures drawn in a simple, local style, without naturalistic details. A few vessels in the large assemblage were painted in the local Late Bronze decorative style with bands, triglyphs and metopes.

The destruction of this building was dated by the pottery to ca. 1400 B.C.E. and may be attributed either to Ameno-phis II's campaign in Canaan or to a local attack on the town.

Fig. 4.9. Scaraboid decorated with Hathor-headed sistrum, Stratum VIII.

Fig. 4.10. Concentration of broken pottery vessels on floor of patrician house storeroom, Stratum VIII (Locus 467).

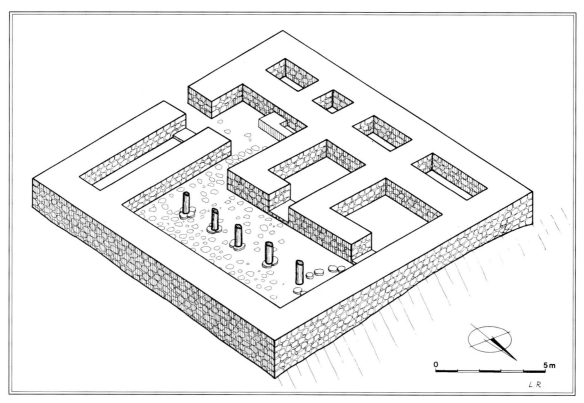

Fig. 4.11. Isometric view of Stratum VIII patrician house in Area B.

Fig. 4.12. General view of floors and walls of Canaanite patrician house, Stratum VIII (view to south).

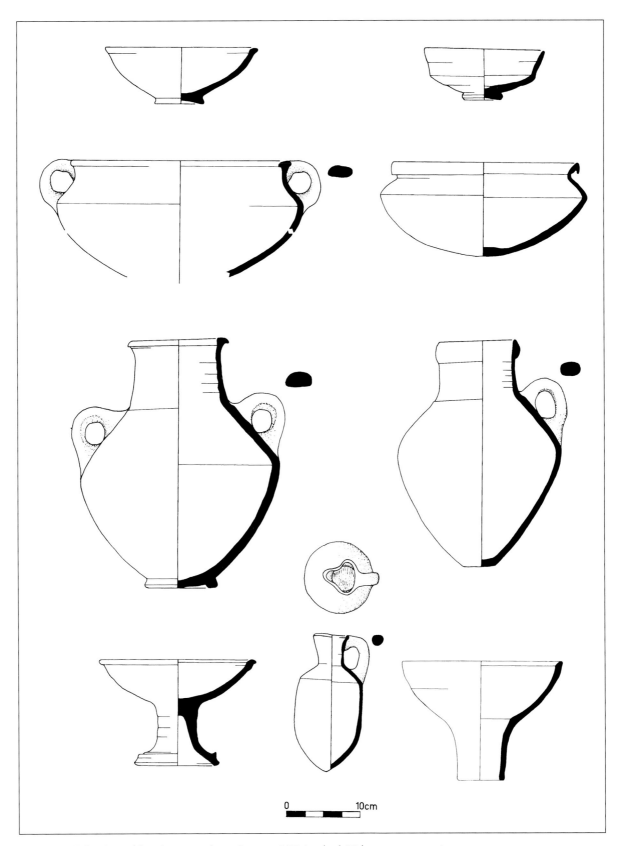

Fig. 4.13. Selection of local pottery from Stratum VIII (end of 15th century B.C.E.).

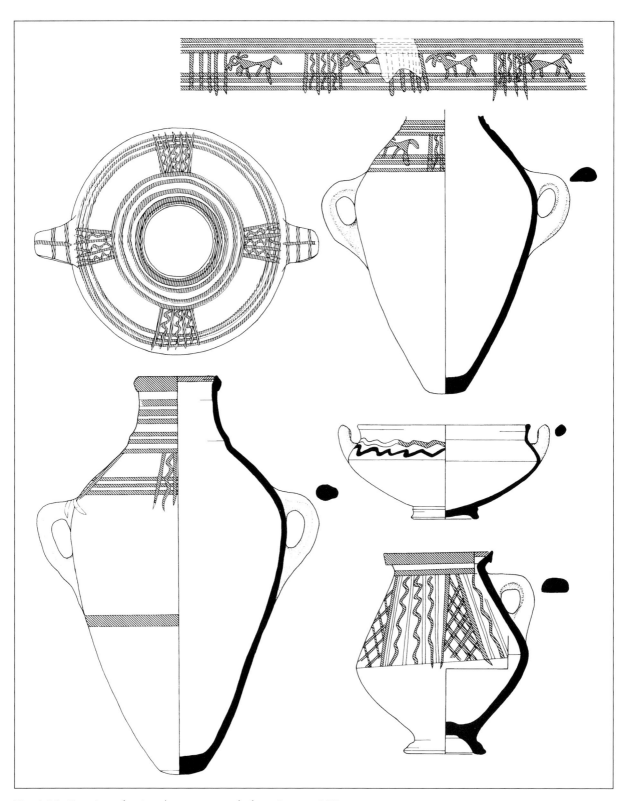

Fig. 4.14. Drawing of painted pottery vessels from Stratum VIII.

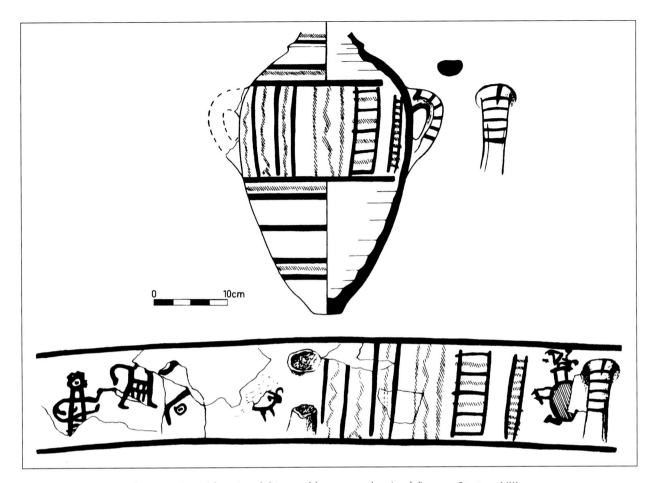

Fig. 4.15. Drawing of storage jar with painted frieze of human and animal figures, Stratum VIII.

The Fourth Canaanite City (Stratum VII)

The final phase of massive architectural structures excavated in Area B was a two-story building that also had been destroyed in a dramatic conflagration. Its brick superstructure had collapsed into a 1.8-m accumulation of brick debris, baked in the intense fire to vivid reds, oranges, and yellows. Remnants of the ceiling, wooden support beams and pillars were found in black charcoal deposits beneath the burnt brick. On the floor, buried beneath the charcoal and ash, a large collection of domestic objects had been crushed by the collapsing building.

The new building (its outer dimensions now 11.3 × 13.2 m) was somewhat smaller than its predecessor. Its outer western wall had been constructed on an inner wall of the Stratum VIII building. This modification excluded the small cells

Opposite, top: Fig. 4.16. General view of Stratum VII building, stone pavement, and pillar bases (view to south); lower walls in the center of the picture belong to the Stratum VIII building (Area B).

Opposite, bottom: Fig. 4.17. General view of Late Bronze building (Stratum VII) with storeroom in narrow corridor in upper right (view to east).

Below: Fig. 4.18. Plan of Late Bronze patrician house (Stratum VII), 14th century B.C.E.

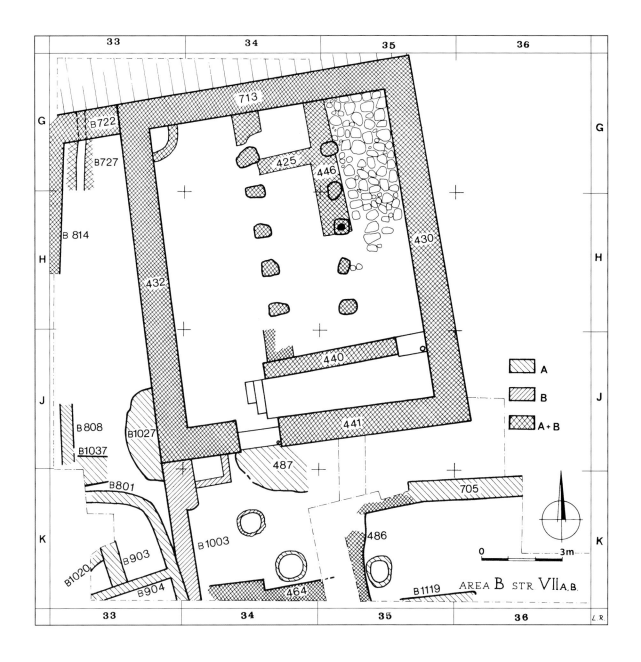

in the western wing of the previous building from the new structure. The outer walls of this building (1.2 m thick) were built of medium-sized stones, with larger stones reinforcing the corners. While significant changes had taken place in the building's plan, walls constructed on stumps of partly-destroyed Stratum VIII walls resulted in the preservation of

Fig. 4.19. Late Bronze mud brick with mason's mark.

Fig. 4.20. Isometric drawing of Stratum VII pillared building in Area B.

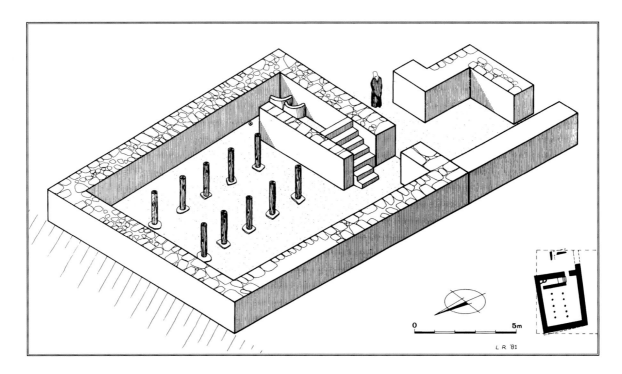

L R '81

Fig. 4.21–22. Patrician House storeroom with three storage jars containing carbonized wheat.

Fig. 4.23. Excavation of storage jars with carbonized grain in storeroom under staircase in patrician house.

Fig. 4.24. A broken jug base with almonds and a fused cluster of bronze objects from storeroom (Stratum VII).

S 437

Fig. 4.25. Storage jar with carbonized grain (Stratum VII).

some features of the previous plan. The location of the main entrance was retained, though at a higher level, and the staircase to the second story used the same narrow corridor as its predecessor. The flat stones of the first three steps of

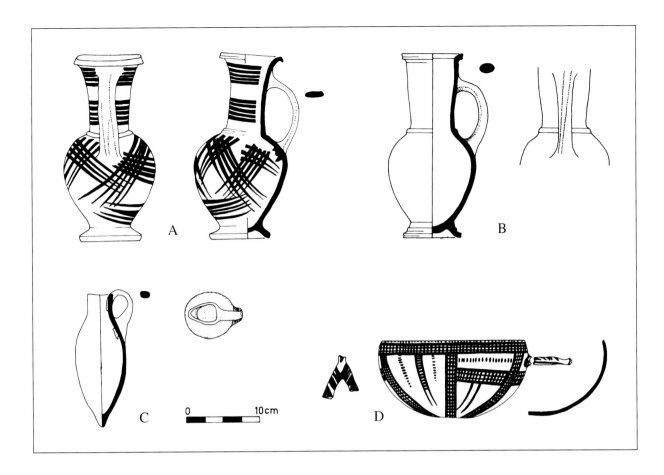

the staircase were still *in situ*. The upper staircase was probably built of wood, an assumption supported by large quantities of black ash found on the floor level of the corridor below the brick rubble. An opening at the other end of the corridor allowed the space below the stairs to be used as a food supply storeroom.

The main feature of the ground floor was a large rectangular hall (9 × 11 m), divided into three elongated sections by two rows of wooden pillars with flat, unworked stone bases. The eastern row of pillar bases consisted of large stone slabs laid on courses of smaller stones embedded in the Stratum VIII destruction layer. The western pillars were supported by a stylobate, a single course stone wall (1.2 m wide) built over the eastern wall of the small chambers of the Stratum VIII building. Thin parallel walls of small stones created narrow compartments between the pillars at the northern end of the eastern row. These support structures and the two rows of pillars bore the second story and subdivided the hall into a central aisle (2.3 m wide) and two

Fig. 4.26. A, C, D: Selection of Cypriot imported pottery from Stratum VII (Area B); B: Local imitation of Cypriot jug.

Fig. 4.27. Storage jar with clay stopper.

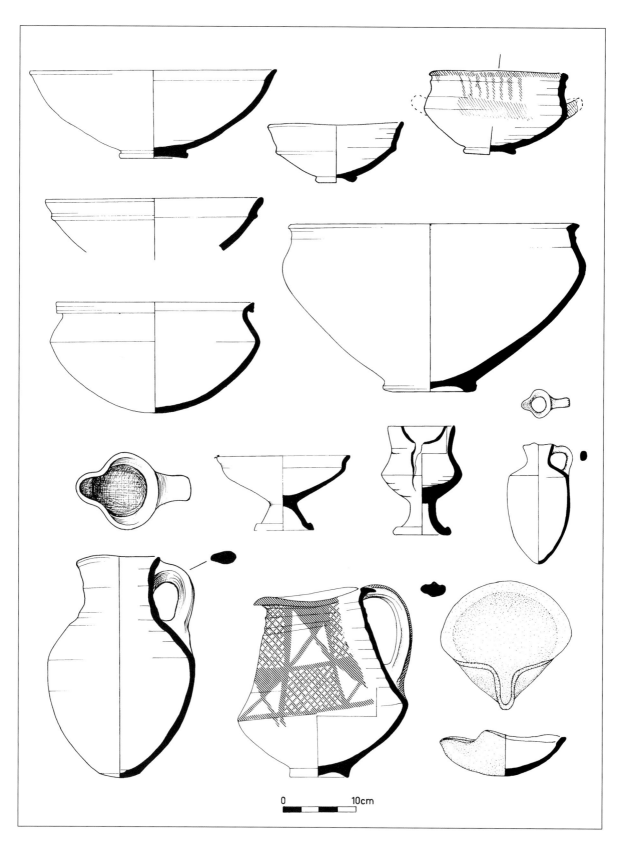

Fig. 4.28. Selection of local pottery from Stratum VII (14th century B.C.E.).

side rooms (2 m on east and 3.5 m on west). A narrow secondary partition wall created an additional small chamber at the northern end of the central passage. The floor was paved with thick white lime plaster on a cobblestone base. A large accumulation of river pebbles along the base of the hall's western wall resulted from the deterioration of the coarse filling (chinking) between the large wall stones used in the smoothing process before plastering. The structure's architectural design and its finds suggest that the lower story served primarily as a service and storage space, while the main living quarters were on the second floor at the top of the staircase.

This architectural plan with two rows of pillars dividing a large rectangular unit has no close parallels among domestic structures of the Late Bronze Age, except in some buildings of poorer construction technique recently excavated at Tel Halif and at Tel Harasim, both in the Shephelah south of Tel Batash. (The building known as the sanctuary excavated by de Vaux at Tell el-Far'ah (N) is another good parallel, although it was probably constructed in the Iron Age I).[6]

The tripartite division of this building seems to anticipate similar architectural features in Iron Age I architecture, like the tripartite division of rectangular buildings found at Tell Abu Hawam, Tell Qasile, and Tel Hadar (all dated to the eleventh century B.C.E.), as well as the use of rows of pillars in dwellings, as at Tel Masos, Tel Qasile, Tel Keisan, and many other sites.[7] This Iron Age architectural style was formerly thought to have no Late Bronze antecedents. It now appears that the pillared houses of Canaanite Timnah and other sites in the Shephelah provide the first evidence for the existence of such architectural traditions in southern Canaan.

Two human skeletons found under the burnt debris of Stratum VII provide evidence of the building's violent end. One lay on the floor in the center of the hall, and the other had fallen over the sill of the hall's entrance, among the fallen bricks from the second floor. These were the remains of two Timnahites who probably were trapped in the fiery collapse of the building.

The destruction debris also contained a fine collection of household wares, possibly typical of such an opulent residence. The finds suggest that the upper story consisted of the main living quarters and possibly a reception room,

Local Canaanite seal featuring an animal procession that includes a gazelle, griffin, and bull, with an eagle and crouching lion above the heads of other animals.

Local Canaanite seal depicting a kneeling figure riding upon the exaggeratedly long back of a deer and two standing figures.

Common Mitannian style seal depicting two standing figures flanking the sacred tree, two deer, and geometric patterns in the lower half of the panel below the deer.

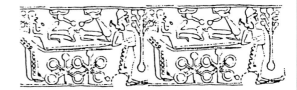

Common Mitannian style seal depicting a seated deity. The figure sits on a low throne and holds a large, knobbed staff topped by a disk in one hand, grasping a bouquet-style sacred tree with the other. A standing deer looks back at the god from the opposite side of the tree.

Cypriot seal of a group almost unknown in Palestine. In addition to portraying a human, a sacred plant, and a crouching animal, this seal also has three signs in the Cypro-Minoan script of the Late Cypriot II period.

Stratum VIIB light faience seal depicting a seated figure on a simple throne with an upraised hand, walking figure, and deer. The seal is likely of local manufacture.

Fig. 4.29. Drawings of cylinder seal impressions from Stratum VII.

while the lower floor provided storage space, cooking facilities, and other domestic services. The finds consisted mainly of storage vessels, cooking pots, metal objects, and some imported Mycenaean and Cypriot pottery. Below the staircase (Locus 437), three of the five storage jars standing along the storeroom walls contained large quantities of carbonized grain. A nearby jug containing almonds, complete in their pulpy outer shells, also contained a fused cluster of bronze arrowheads and other bronze objects. A large Cypriot "bilbil" jug of the so-called Base-Ring II group also was found in the storeroom. Scattered on the floor of the main hall were many broken jars, bowls, and cooking pots, most distorted by the intense heat of the fire. This collection included a complete Mycenaean pyxis of the Mycenaean IIIA2 family and an intact bull-shaped vessel of Cypriot Base-Ring II ware. This pottery assemblage and other objects found in the building have been dated to the fourteenth century B.C.E. Spearheads, arrowheads, and chisels, all made of bronze, also were found on this floor. Domestic objects in use on the second floor and possible personal effects of the house owner were found in the fallen debris in the south-western corner of the hall. Of special interest were approximately fifty beads, mostly made of glass, five cylinder seals, two Egyptian seals, and bronze cymbals.

Two of the cylinder seals represent the "Common Mitannian style," depicting worshippers, trees, and animals in characteristic style. One is a genuine Mitannian seal, typical of the fifteenth–early fourteenth centuries B.C.E., while the other is a "degenerate" version, commonly found in Canaan during the Late Bronze Age II in both fourteenth- and thir-teenth-century-B.C.E. contexts.[8] A third seal is of a Cypriot group almost unknown in Palestine. In addition to portraying a human, a sacred plant, and a crouching animal, this seal also bears three signs in the Cypro-Minoan script of the Late Cypriot II period. The other two cylinders are carved in peculiar local Canaanite styles, paralleled on only a few other seals, depicting combinations of animals and humans. These five cylinder seals thus form an important collection representing the glyptic styles common in a Late Bronze context, particularly in the fourteenth century B.C.E.[9]

The presence of Egyptian scarabs at Timnah is equally interesting. The use of scarabs as seals within Egypt certi-fied the contents of containers, bound commodities, and en-veloped or tied written documents. Scarabs inscribed with the royal cartouche implied the authority of the pharaoh. In regions of Egyptian jurisdiction, royal scarabs may have been tokens of administrative or diplomatic recognition for authenticating official negotiations and agreements leading to commercial and political treaties. Many scarabs, without

Fig. 4.30. Ptah seal.

Fig. 4.31. Two-sided steatite seal, Stratum VII.

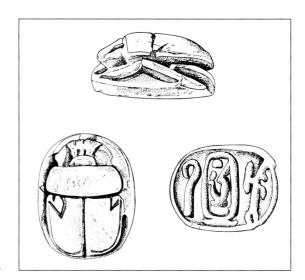

Fig. 4.32. Scarab with cartouche of Amenophis III.

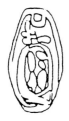

Fig. 4.33. Scaraboid of Queen Tiy, inscribed "Royal Wife, Great One, Tiy."

any practical function, however, were valued as precious objects. The Egyptian seals found at Timnah include a scarab with the cartouche of Amenophis III and a scaraboid with the cartouche of his consort, Queen Tiy, providing a *terminus post quem* for the destruction of the building at the beginning of the fourteenth century B.C.E.

This impressive dwelling, like its predecessor, may have been the home of a wealthy family, perhaps landowners in the Sorek Valley. Its destruction in a fierce conflagration occurred during the fourteenth century B.C.E., probably as the result of conflicts between rival cities or an attack by *Habiru* gangs of the type documented in the Amarna letters. These letters provide ample documentation of internecine rivalries, which seem to have been common during a temporary lapse of direct Egyptian surveillance over the Canaanite city-states. Such a situation would undoubtedly have provided an adequate incentive for a challenge of territorial rights over the desirable lands surrounding Timnah.[10] The fiery destruction of towns, such as Timnah, during this period may be attributed to local aspirations, when seeming opportunities for encroachment in surrounding territories ended in failure or unexpected Egyptian retribution.

The building described above was probably only part of a larger complex. A small courtyard (4 × 5 m) south of the building was used for domestic activities, such as baking in clay ovens. It may have been an inner courtyard, bounded by structures on the west and south and entered through a

2-m-wide alley from the east, where other Late Bronze buildings may have been built down the slope of the mound. The debris in the courtyard consisted of layers of decayed organic material, ash from cleaning ovens, and the periodic deposition of burnt garbage, resulting in alternating layers of gray ashy earth and black ash. Evidence of successive re-paving suggests that the courtyard was in use for an extended period, while the main building continued to exist without significant modification. Regular repaving raised the courtyard floors 0.7 m, while the floor of the main building remained unchanged. This was a phenomenon typical in Middle Eastern cities and towns, where buildings were used over long periods with no major structural changes while the surfaces of the associated open spaces and courtyards were continuously raised.

Only small areas of the buildings to the south and east of the courtyard were excavated. Two successive construction phases were defined in this area, both contemporary with the main building. In the first phase (VIIB), a large

Fig. 4.34. Volunteer excavating in Area B.

baking oven (1 m in diameter) dominated the center of the courtyard. A narrow stone wall, built as a continuation of the western wall of the main building, enclosed the courtyard on the west. A plastered structure at the eastern end of the courtyard appears to have been part of an industrial installation. Though its precise function is obscure, it may have been used for processing agricultural products.

In the second phase (VIIA), the courtyard's floor and the entrance to the building were raised, a new oven replaced the earlier one at the southern end of the courtyard and a new wall bounded the courtyard on the south. To the east of the courtyard (in the southeastern quadrant of Area B), only a corner of a newly constructed building was exposed. A large monolithic trough (1 m in diameter) that stood in this corner may have been used for processing olives or some other agricultural product.

In the southwestern corner of Area B, the wall enclosing the courtyard during Phase VIIB was removed in Phase VIIA to make way for the construction of a new, rather poor structure with thin walls only one stone thick. A rounded corner and two partition walls of this structure were exposed. It was perhaps an auxiliary structure or servants' dwelling related to the main Stratum VII building. These two structures of Phase VIIA were destroyed in an intense fire.

The area west of the main building of Stratum VII became a street or alley, ca. 2.6 m wide. On the western side of the street, the outer wall of an adjacent building was exposed, although the building itself was not excavated. Accumulations of gray organic materials and ash, typical of open spaces, were found in this alley. The alley between the two large buildings, with an open drainage channel, was blocked by a wall at the edge of the mound to preserve the continuous perimeter wall. The city thus relied on the outer walls of the peripheral buildings to compensate for the absence of a genuine city wall. The drainage channel pierced the wall through a narrow opening roofed with large flat stones. The street had apparently been used during all three phases of Stratum VII.

An interesting object found in the Stratum VII street debris was an intact clay Astarte figurine plaque. The nude goddess is portrayed in a standing frontal position with feet turned aside and holding two papyrus plants. The figure,

Fig. 4.35. Astarte plaque figurine from Stratum VII.

which has no facial features, has a Hathor coiffure with the ears exposed and three bracelets adorning her wrists and ankles. Her body has a narrow waist and wide hips, with the pubic area emphasized by a deeply incised triangle. It is interesting to note that two fragments of similar figurines, made from the same mold, were purchased a long time ago by the Israel Department of Antiquities and are now exhibited in the Israel Museum. Incised facial features had been added to these figures. This indicates that facial features, lacking in the original mold, were added to the individual figurine after casting. In the case of the figurine from Tel Batash, these details were never finished.

A Period of Decline: The Thirteenth Century B.C.E. (Stratum VI)

The four successive strata of the sixteenth-fourteenth centuries B.C.E., each with its patrician dwellings destroyed in a violent conflagration, ended during the fourteenth century B.C.E. The subsequent and final phase of Canaanite Timnah (Stratum VI) defies adequate description, since only a few building remains of this phase were preserved.

In the southeastern corner of Area B, two building phases of this period were detected. In the earlier phase (Stratum VIB), a new building replaced the building of Phase VIIA. Only a corner formed by two massive walls enclosing a stone floor was exposed, with a thin destruction layer. The continuation of this building was found just below the surface in an Area J probe (south of Area B), which was not fully excavated. A courtyard with a small stone trough lay to the west of this building, extending at least 10 m to the west.

In the second phase (Stratum VIA), a dwelling with massive stone foundations replaced the previous building. This building, 9.8 m long and approximately 8.5 m wide, had a large hall or an open courtyard and two or three additional rooms. Few pottery sherds were found on its cobblestone and earth floors, indicating a date at the end of the Late Bronze Age. No evidence was found for a violent end of this building. On the contrary, it was reused by the Philistines in the following period.

In Area B's northwest quadrant, the corner of a second building was exposed above the remains of the ruined Stratum VII building. The floors of this stratum yielded very few finds. The pottery sherds are of types characteristic of the Late Bronze Age II. The *terminus ante quem* for the end of this stratum was the Philistine pottery that characterizes the next stratum. It may be assumed that this last Canaanite city came to its end during the second half of the thirteenth century. This stratum appears to represent a period of decline in Timnah's history, which lasted for most of the

Fig. 4.36. General view of architectural remains of Strata VII and VI in Area B (looking north).

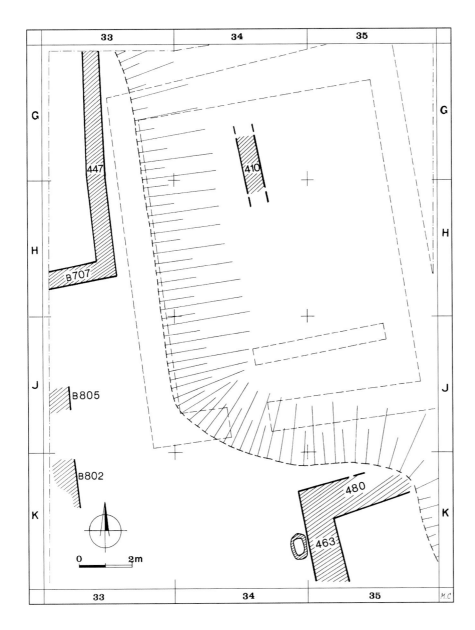

Fig. 4.37. Fragmentary architectural remains of Stratum VIB in Area B.

thirteenth century B.C.E. There is evidence for destruction by fire at the end of Phase VIB in the southern building, though no total and violent destruction of the city seems to have occurred at the end of this period Stratum VIA, and thus the Late Bronze phase appears to end peacefully.

Late Bronze Remains in Area A

Successive Canaanite buildings of the Late Bronze Age also were found in the narrow trench (Area A) on the northern slope of the mound. A few remains of Strata X and IX were detected there above the Middle Bronze rampart. Higher up, a 1.1-m-thick outer wall from a large building, running parallel to the tell's slope, was preserved to a height of 1.5 m. Four of its six courses were tilted outward as a result of erosion pressure along the steep slope.

Subphases of reconstruction within the wall and the replastering of floors reflected at least four to five occupational phases. A destruction layer toward the end of the period, which can be correlated with the end of Stratum VII in Area B, yielded a collection of pottery vessels including a small painted storage jar and a Cypriot Base-Ring II "bilbil" jug. The limited extent of excavation within the section precluded a definite determination of the building's character or purpose, but it appears to be a patrician house similar to the one in Area B. Its massive outer wall and its extended use during successive occupational phases suggest a substantial structure, perhaps an extension of the "acropolis" complex partly excavated in Area B. Its construction phases probably paralleled Strata VIII–VII in Area B. The subsequent phase, including a segment of a narrow partition wall and a thin floor, seems to be equivalent to Stratum VI in Area B.

Late Bronze Remains in Area C

A few building remains of the Late Bronze Age have been identified below the Iron Age gate in the deepest probes in Area C. The fragmentary remains appear to belong to two large buildings erected along the crest of the mound, similar to the buildings on the mound's crest in Areas A and B. A 4.1-m-wide passage with a drainage channel along its edge passed between these buildings leading into the city. A massive diagonal wall erected on the slope of the mound opposite the passage may have been a retaining wall for the approach ramp into the city. These remains, scant as they are, provide evidence of the nature of the town entrance during this period; even though there was probably no actual city gate structure, there was a planned wide entrance leading through a perimeter of adjoining buildings. Such an arrangement at Timnah is consistent with the general nature of Late Bronze towns without an adequate fortification

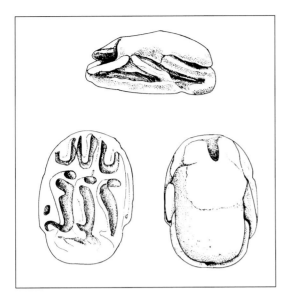

Fig. 4.38. Faience scarab featuring three standing cobras (*uraei*), a design common during the Eighteenth Dynasty (from a mixed locus of Iron I and Late Bronze II in Area C).

system, which depended on the outer walls of a continuous line of massive buildings as their only defense.

The accumulated data from Areas A, B and C have revealed the basic features of the stratigraphy, continuous changes and city planning of the Late Bronze town at Tel Batash. The excavation of Area B has revealed the existence of five Late Bronze strata. Thus Timnah has provided one of the most detailed successions of strata for the Late Bronze Age in southern Palestine and offers an opportunity for extensive excavation in the future, as well as for continued study of the cultural phenomena of this period. In the four earlier strata, spanning a period of about 200 years (ca. 1550–1350 B.C.E.), the northeastern corner of the town contained patrician houses exhibiting architectural continuity and durability. Most of the outer walls of these houses survived four major conflagrations and served four distinct periods of occupation. All four buildings were destroyed by intense fire, reflecting the unstable political situation in the region during this period.

In spite of four consecutive conflagrations at Timnah between the mid-sixteenth and the fourteenth centuries B.C.E., its citizens quickly rebuilt the town after each disaster, and the local Canaanite culture exhibits a tenacious continuity. During this period the town appears to have been a part of the city-state of Gezer, and though vulnerable to attacks, its economic and political backing were sufficient for speedy

Table 4.2. Chronological Correlation of Timnah's Late Bronze Stratigraphic Sequence

Period	Dates	Strata	Egyptian Chronology
LB IA	1550 B.C.E.	X	
LB I B	1470 B.C.E.	IX VIII	Thutmosis III Amenophis II
LB IIA	1400 B.C.E.	VIIB VIIA	 Amarna Period
LB IIB	1300 B.C.E. 1200 B.C.E.	VIB VIA	Ramesses II Merneptah

recovery. The cultural vitality in the Shephelah stands in sharp contrast to the situation in the country's peripheral areas like the northern Negev and the central hill country, where Late Bronze occupation was rather poor.

The thirteenth century B.C.E. appears to be a period of decline for the kingdom of Gezer.[11] Gezer itself was quite poor during this period, and Timnah only partly recovered from the devastating blows received during the fourteenth century B.C.E.

The end of Late Bronze Timnah stands in contrast to the events at Lachish in the southern Shephelah.[12] The destruction of Lachish VII by fire at the end of the thirteenth century B.C.E. was followed by the rebuilding of the city during the early twelfth century B.C.E. (Lachish VI). This new city retained a strong Egyptian influence and possible occupation during the time of the Twentieth Dynasty. It was totally destroyed by fire about the mid-twelfth century, abandoned, and left desolate for a long time. The fate of Timnah was quite different. We cannot say whether the last Canaanite city (Stratum VIA) survived during the early twelfth century B.C.E. The town appears to have disintegrated slowly and was ultimately abandoned until it was reoccupied by Philistines in the latter part of the twelfth century B.C.E.

Endnotes

1. J. M. Weinstein, "The Egyptian Empire in Palestine: A Reassessment." *BASOR* 241 (1981) 1–10; D. B. Redford, *Egypt, Canaan, and Israel in Ancient Times* (Princeton, 1992) 125–240.

2. A. Kempinski, "Tell el-ᶜAjjul—Beth-Aglayim or Sharuhen?" *IEJ* 24 (1974) 145–52.

3. We use the name "Timnah" in this chapter with reservations: we really do not know the name of the Canaanite town (before the Iron Age).

4. I. Singer, "Merneptah's Campaign to Canaan and the Egyptian Occupation of the Southern Coastal Plain of Palestine in the Ramesside Period," *BASOR* 269 (1988) 1–10.

5. For divergent views, see S. Ahituv, "Economic Factors in the Egyptian Conquest of Canaan," *IEJ* 28 (1978) 93–105; N. Na'aman, "Economic Aspects of the Egyptian Occupation of Canaan," *IEJ* 31 (1981) 172–85.

6. S. Giveon, *The Third Season of Excavation at Tel Harasim, 1992: Preliminary Report No. 3* (Tel Aviv, 1993) figs. 8–9; R. de Vaux, "Les Fouilles de Tell el-Farᵓah pres Naplouse," *Revue Biblique* 64 (1957) 574–77.

7. For summaries and references, see A. Kempinski and R. Reich (eds.), *The Architecture of Ancient Israel* (Jerusalem, 1992) 193–99, 223–28; on Tel Hadar, see M. Kochavi, "The Land of Geshur Project, 1989–1990," Notes and News, *IEJ* 41 (1991) 180–84.

8. H.J. Kantor, *Soundings at Tell Fakhariyah* (Oriental Institute Publications 79; Chicago: University of Chicago, 1958) 82–85.

9. D. C. Maltsberger, *Glyptic Remains from Timnah: Geopolitical and Socioeconomic Implications for the Shephelah During the Amarna Period.* (Unpublished dissertation; Fort Worth, Tx.: Southwestern Baptist Theological Seminary, 1992) 162–65.

10. J. M. Weinstein, "The Egyptian Empire in Palestine," 1–28; P. A. Bienkowski, "Prosperity and Decline in LBA Canaan: A Reply to Liebowitz and Knapp," *BASOR* 276 (1989) 59–63; R. Gonen, "Urban Canaan in the Late Bronze Period," *BASOR* 253 (1984) 61–73.

11. W. G. Dever (ed.), *Gezer IV* (Jerusalem, 1986) 51–60.

12. D. Ussishkin, "Levels VII and VI at Tell Lachish and the End of the Late Bronze Age in Canaan," *Palestine in the Bronze and Iron Ages: Papers in Honour of Olga Tufnell* (ed. J.N.Tubb; London, 1985) 213–30.

Fig. C1. Aerial view of Tel Batash (Timnah) on the southern bank of the Brook Sorek (Excavation areas concentrated in the northeastern quadrant).

Fig. C2. Early field work in progress at Tel Batash (1978 season).

Fig. C3 (left, above). Area A step-trench on northern slope of tell.
Fig. C4 (right above). Trench cutting through the earthen rampart to the outer face of the Middle Bronze fortifications near northeastern corner of the mound (Area B, looking south).
Fig. C5 (below). General view of patrician houses in Area B (looking north, at end of 1988 season).

Fig. C6. Late Bronze painted pottery vessels from Area B (Stratum VIII).

Fig. C7. Storage jars from patrician house storeroom.

Fig. C8 (right). Astarte plaque figurine from Stratum VII.

Fig. C9. A broken jug base with almonds and a fused cluster of bronze objects from storeroom (Stratum VII).

Fig. C10. A Mycenaean pyxis from the Late Bronze building in Area B (Stratum VII).

Fig. C11. Cypriot Base-Ring zoomorphic vessel from Stratum VII (Area B).

Fig. C12. Bronze objects from Stratum VII destruction debris: daggers, arrowheads, spearhead, chisels, cymbal and pins.

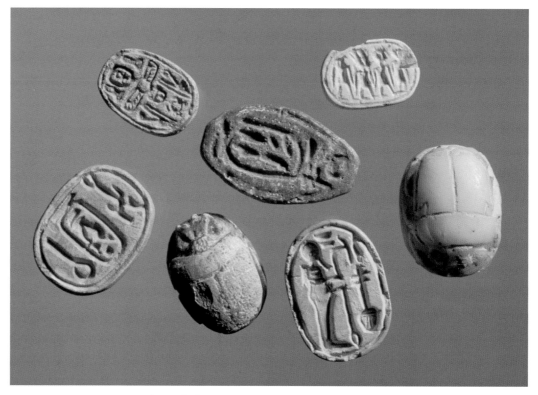

Fig. C13. Late Bronze scarabs including a cartouche of Amenophis III and scaraboid of Queen Tiy, inscribed "Royal Wife, Great One, Tiy."

Fig. C14 (left). Cypriot jug of the "white shaved" family, in the form of a Syrian flask.

Fig. C15 (below). A faience, glass and stone-bead necklace and cylinder seals from the Late Bronze II building in Area B.

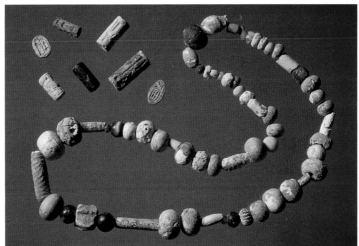

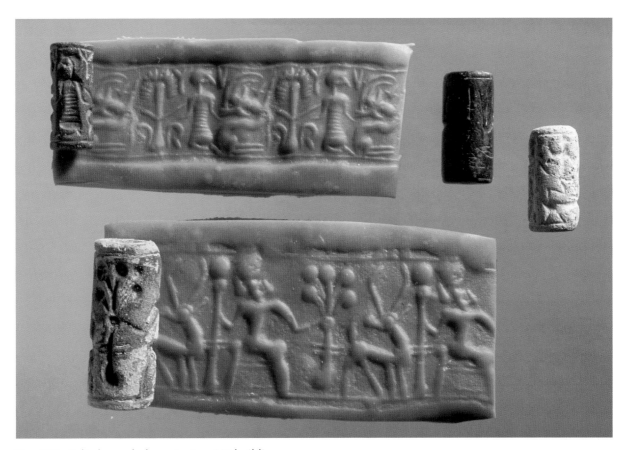

Fig. C16. Cylinder seals from Stratum VII building.

Fig C17. Architectural remains of Philistine Timnah.

Fig. C18 (below). Philistine pyramidal-shaped seal depicting a lyre player.

Fig. C19 (right). Clay bull's head from Stratum V.

Fig. C20 (left). Ceramic *'Cyrano'* head from Philistine period (Stratum V). This figurine retains Aegean and Cypriot traditions.

Fig. C21 (above). Typical painted "Philistine" pottery and sherds (Stratum V).

Fig C22. General view of gate area excavations (Area C). Note course of drainage channel (left center).

Fig. C23. Typical *lmlk* storage jar and scoops.

Fig. C24 (below). Storage jar handle with four-winged *lmlk* sealing. (Area D).

Fig. C25 (right). Storage jar handle with two-winged *lmlk mmst* sealing.

Fig. C26. Chalices from cultic corner in Area E (Stratum II).

Fig. C27. General view of Area D, showing remains of storage building of Stratum III superimposed by a seventh century B.C.E. building of Stratum II. The Iron Age II city wall is seen along the northern crest of the mound (looking north).

Fig. C28. General view of Iron Age II buildings (foreground) in Areas D and E (view to east).

Fig. C29. Oil press installation in the "Oil Press Building" in Area E (Stratum II).

Fig. C30. Architect's drawing of oil press installation in Area E.

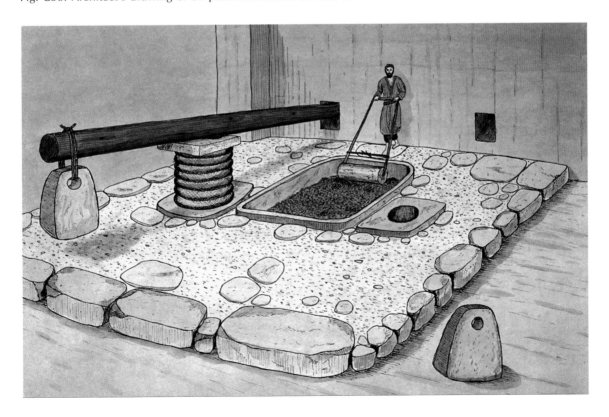

Figs. C31–33. Three clay molds found in Area E with the female figurines cast from them (Stratum III).

Fig. C34. General view of Area H (Strata III-II).

Fig. C35. Linda and Gary Goad, excavators of Area H oil press complex, preparing the area for photography.

Fig. C36 (above, left). Amphora from Area F (Stratum II)

Fig. C37 (above, right). A storage jar from the end of the Iron Age or the Persian period.

Fig. C38 (below). Series of commercial weights of Judean type (*pym* and *shekel* units) (Stratum II).

5 Philistine Timnah

Historical Setting

Dramatic ethnic and cultural changes marked the beginning of the Iron Age in Palestine. The homogeneity of Canaan's political and economic city-state structure had been fragmented by the incursion of various ethnic groups and the decline of Egyptian administrative and military control. The Canaanite population in Palestine proper was forced to defend itself against the Philistines and other "Sea Peoples" in the coastal plains, while in the central hill country the Israelite tribes settled and founded hundreds of new settlements. The Iron Age I can be divided into two cultural phases: Iron Age IA (1200–1150 B.C.E.), contemporary with Egypt's Twentieth Dynasty, saw continued Egyptian domination and a continuation of a thriving Canaanite culture in many parts of the country. However, the arrival of the "Sea Peoples" and the disruption of international trade signaled the onset of a significant change in the region. The Iron Age IB (1150–1000 B.C.E.), contemporary with the Twenty-first Dynasty, included the demise of Egyptian control, the consolidation of Philistine control in the southern coastal region, and the period of Israelite integration known as the period of the Judges.[1]

The Late Bronze–Iron Age transition at Timnah clearly represents this major cultural break. Though the circumstances that brought an end to Canaanite Timnah are unknown, it is clear that the last Canaanite town (Stratum VI) represents a period of decline, perhaps followed by an occupational gap. It is also possible that Stratum VI represents the continuity of Canaanite life within the fringe area beyond immediate Philistine settlement during the period of Philistine consolidation and the establishment of their "pentapolis" during the first half of the twelfth century B.C.E. However, with the growth of nearby Ekron (Tel Miqne)—the main Philistine city in the region—the expansion of the Philistines into the neighboring Sorek Valley and the expulsion of Timnah's Canaanite population were almost inevitable.

Fig. 5.1. Map: Eastern expansion of the Sea Peoples "by land and by sea."

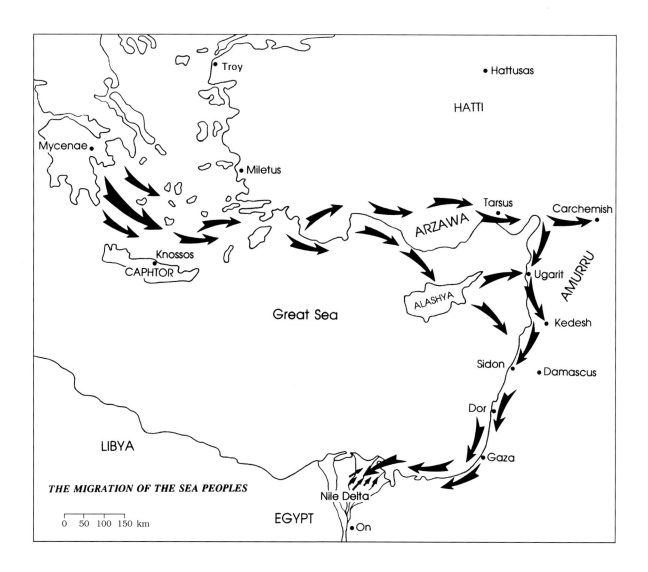

THE MIGRATION OF THE SEA PEOPLES

0   50 100 150 km

Philistine Timnah was probably founded as a satellite of Ekron. However, it is possible that the Philistine population of the town consisted mainly of overlords and aristocrats, while the lower classes were descendants of the earlier Canaanite inhabitants who had succumbed to Philistine control. Such a scenario is consistent with the basic features characterizing the Stratum VI–V transition.

The Biblical Perspective

Israelite occupation in the central hill country during the Late Bronze-Iron Age transition contributed to territorial conflicts and ethnic tensions in the Shephelah. The settlement of the Danites in the northern Shephelah and coastal plain is described in the biblical narratives in less than glowing terms.

> The Amorites pressed the Danites back into the hill country, for they did not allow them to come down to the plain; the Amorites persisted in dwelling in Har-heres, in Aijalon, and in Shaalbim, . . . (Judg 1:34).

Danite settlement is identified with Eshtaol and Zorah (the birthplace of Samson), situated on a spur overlooking the eastern part of the Sorek Valley. The superior strength of the indigenous *Amorites* precluded occupation of the rich alluvial valleys in the immediate vicinity. This may provide some explanation for the biblical reference to a *Mahaneh-Dan* ("camp of Dan"), a temporary settlement of the frustrated Danites awaiting access to the territories in the northern Shephelah and coastal plain supposedly intended as part of their tribal inheritance.

The introduction of the Samson narratives suggests that the successful settlement of the Danites in the northern Shephelah was complicated further by the arrival of the Philistines.

> . . . the Lord gave them ("the people of Israel") into the hand of the Philistines for forty years (Judg 13:1).

It is within this context that the biblical narratives of the exploits of the Danite judge Samson are set. The topographical and geographical implications of biblical references to Timnah and its region, especially in the life of Samson (Judges 14–15), fit in well with its identification with Tel

Batash. The life and exploits of Samson of Zorah, the Danite village located on a ridge 7 km east of Tel Batash, while suggesting social interaction by individuals and families, dramatically portray the political tensions that existed along the Philistine-Israelite border between the two towns.

> Samson went down to Timnah, and at Timnah he saw one of the daughters of the Philistines. Then he came up, and told his father and mother, "I saw one of the daughters of the Philistines at Timnah; now get her for me as my wife." But his father and mother said to him, "Is there not a woman among the daughters of your kinsmen, or among all our people, that you must go to take a wife from the uncircumcised Philistines?" But Samson said to his father, "Get her for me; for she pleased me well." His father and mother did not know that it was from the Lord; for he was seeking an occasion against the Philistines. At that time the Philistines had dominion over Israel. Then Samson went down with his father and mother to Timnah, . . . (Judg 14:1–5)

The account of Samson's heroic acts in Timnah and its environs is filled with action and intrigue. His romance, courtship, and subsequent marriage to the Timnahite girl provides the biblical pretext of his personal troubles with the Philistines. The graphic biblical description of Samson's exploits and heroism in the killing of thirty Ashkelonites (Judg 14:10–19), the torching of Timnah's wheatfields and olive orchards (Judg 15:4–5), and his *great slaughter* at Timnah to avenge the death of his in-laws (Judg 15:6–8) seemingly are representative episodes reflecting the ethnic and territorial struggles within the buffer zone of the Shephelah during the period of the Judges. The portrayal of his personal valor is interwoven with the duplicity of his Philistine wife and betrayal of his Judean kinsmen. The biblical account clearly portrays the Philistines as the dominant force in this territorial conflict and the Judahites' fear of Philistine retaliation as a result of Samson's actions. To avert Philistine retribution, Samson's kinsmen, before physically delivering him to their enemies, challenged the nature of his conduct:

> Do you not know that the Philistines are rulers over us? What then is this that you have done to us? (Judg 15:11)

Subsequent biblical discussion of the tribe of Dan implies that Samson's efforts failed to achieve any territorial gains

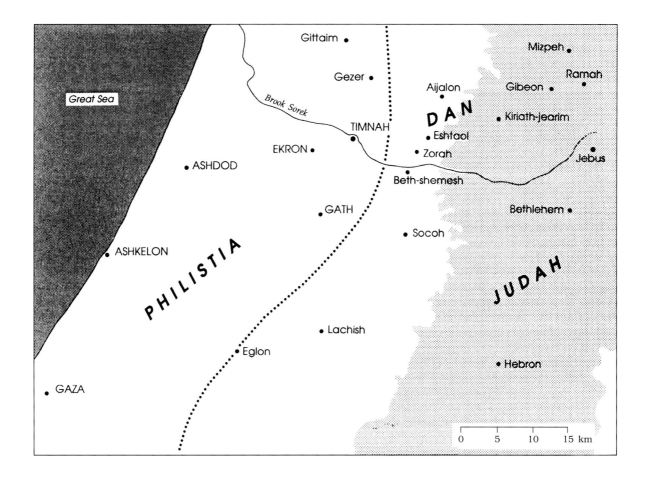

Fig. 5.2. Map: Judah–Philistia border during the period of Samson.

along the Philistine frontier and ultimately, apart from the towns of Zorah and Eshtaol, the Danites were forced to seek additional settlement opportunities elsewhere (Judges 18).

The Philistine Town (Stratum V)

The Philistine town appears to have been a well-established, fortified urban center. Unfortunately, only small portions of it were exposed by the excavations. In the northern half of Area B, the remains of the Philistine city had been completely destroyed by erosion. The remains in the area's southern half, however, provided enough material for a basic understanding of the stratigraphy and architecture of the Iron Age I Philistine city.

In the southern part of Area B, the last Canaanite building, that of Stratum VIA, was rehabilitated. The outer walls of the building remained as they had been in the previous period, though new partition walls were constructed and a

Fig. 5.3. Sketch of Egyptians and Sea Peoples in naval combat, possibly in the Nile Delta (from reliefs on Ramesses III's mortuary temple at Medinet Habu).

Fig. 5.4. Stratum V building in Area B, looking north.

new cobble floor was laid in some of the rooms. A somewhat similar building was uncovered by W. F. Albright at Tell Beit Mirsim, in the southern Shephelah (Stratum B2).[2] There, too, the Iron Age I building is a rebuilt older building of the Late Bronze Age (Stratum C).

The finds in our building, although scarce, included characteristic Iron Age I pottery together with some painted Philistine sherds and a clay bull's head, apparently part of a larger cult object.

An open area to the west and northwest of this building was used for cooking and for rubbish pits. Two large baking ovens (*tabuns*) were constructed over the ruined walls of Stratum VI, indicating a major architectural change between the two levels in this particular location. To the south and west of these ovens, six pits had been cut through the accumulation of previous strata. These pits, 1.5–2.0 m in diameter, without finished walls, contained layers of soft gray ashy material. Decayed rubbish and ashes from periodic cleaning of the ovens nearby appeared to make up these pit deposits. To the south and west of the pits, the repeated repair of successive floors and ovens in an open courtyard provided evidence for the town's longevity. A narrow wall,

Fig. 5.5. Stratum V building with pits in foreground in Area B.

Fig. 5.6. Philistine sealing on a bulla retains the impressions of the knotted cord ends it sealed. Probably produced with a conical seal, the impression depicts a schematic human and animal figure.

probably a part of another building, enclosed the open area on the west.

The courtyard and pits yielded some significant finds. A pyramidal limestone seal, perforated at its point, is typical of the period. The scene engraved on it, though highly stylized and incomplete, seems to portray a seated human figure playing a lyre. It resembles a Philistine seal from Ashdod.[3] Another Philistine sealing on a clay bulla retains the impressions of the knotted cord ends it sealed. Probably produced with a conical seal, the impression shows schematic figures of a human and an animal, displaying a close stylistic resemblance to a seal found in Stratum X at Tell Qasile.[4] These two pieces illustrate the existence and nature of Philistine glyptic art, already known from other sites. The bulla indicates that writing on papyrus was practiced by the Philistines during this period, even though this fact has not been documented at other sites. Knowledge of writing dur-

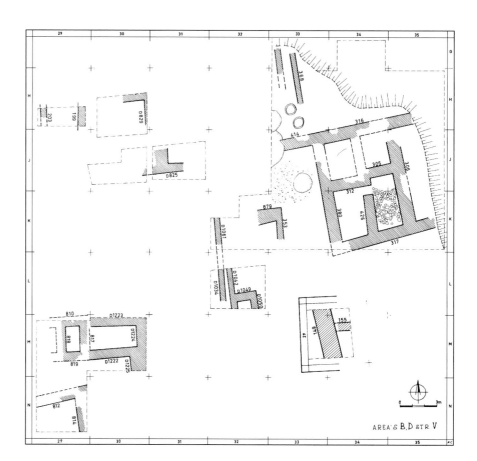

Fig. 5.7. Architectural remains of Philistine Timnah in Areas B and D.

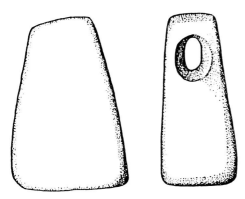

Fig. 5.8. Philistine pyramidal-shaped seal depicting a lyre player.

ing the Philistine period is also demonstrated by a storage jar handle that was incised with a sign identical to the Proto-Canaanite letter "*k*" (*kaph*). It is impossible to judge, however, whether this single sign was a potter's mark or a Proto-Canaanite letter like a similar sign incised on a Late Bronze jar handle from Tell el-ᶜAjjul.[5]

Only fragmentary remains of Stratum V were exposed in Areas D and E. Excavation below tenth century B.C.E. floor levels of Stratum IV in the eastern portion of Area D exposed an open area of Stratum V, a possible continuation of the open area in Area B. In a southern extension of Area D, parts of well-built Philistine buildings made of distinctive yellowish bricks were exposed. In the northern portion of Area D, two brick walls running north-south were exposed below the foundations of the later Iron Age II city wall. These walls indicate that Philistine buildings extended to the edges of the mound.

In the upper part of the stepped trench in Area A (in Square G-29), a massive outer wall (1.45 m thick) of a large building was found, with three courses of stones overlaid by a mudbrick superstructure (one course of which was preserved). Inside this wall, a partition divided a room with a thick plastered floor and a square installation, which had a floor consisting of a 10-cm-thick waterproof layer of hard white lime on a stone foundation. The installation is 1.2 m wide, with a low plastered parapet designed to hold water. A channel permitted drainage through the foundation of the wall along the slope. This drainage channel and the outer

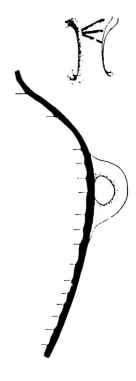

Fig. 5.9. Incised storage jar handle with sign identical to the Proto-Canaanite letter "k" (*kaph*).

surface of the wall below the channel were plastered to protect the wall's foundation against water damage. The installation may have been intended for personal (bathing) or industrial use. The paucity of ceramic finds leaves the date of this later building unclear. It may have been a part of the final Canaanite occupation (Stratum VI) or the Philistine city (Stratum V, though it must be admitted that no Philistine pottery was found in this building). The outer walls of this building may have been part of the outer fortification wall of the Philistine town, which was detected in Area C.

The most interesting discoveries concerning the Philistine city came from beneath the Iron Age II city gates in Area C. Part of a large structure was exposed there, which consisted of a series of brick walls on stone foundations 1.2 to 1.7 m wide. This rectangular structure, at least 14.5 m long and 9.4 m wide, was situated near the crest of the mound and subdivided into smaller rectangular and square chambers. An eastern projection, 4 m long, has been only partly excavated. Its rooms apparently contained an artifi-

Fig. 5.10. General view of gate area excavations (Area C); note course of drainage channel (left center).

cial fill of brick material. The rectangular structure seems to have been incorporated into the fortification system of the Philistine town, though its specific function remains unclear. It covered remains of the Late Bronze city entrance and was covered in turn by the foundations of the Iron Age city gate. It was not a city gate, however, since no architectural evidence of an entrance to the city was found. Its attachment to the city wall would suggest a defensive role for this structure. An administrative or other utilitarian purpose as a part of a greater gate complex may be supported by the consistent tradition of subsequent Iron Age gate construction in this location.

A 1.6-m-wide brick wall extending 7.5 m south of this rectangular building along the eastern crest of the mound may have been a defensive wall, comparable to the massive wall in Area A. This wall extended southward to a rectangular tower 5.5 m long. Three complete Iron Age I vessels from the floor of a trapezoidal room adjoining the rectangular structure and the city wall provided the best evidence for dating the whole complex. It thus appears that the Philistine town was fortified with a relatively weak and unimpressive city wall.

A gabled drainage channel, running east-west, remains a stratigraphic riddle. The channel was exposed for a length of 22 m, with two segments of 3.0 m and 9.5 m excavated on the slope of the tell. Its walls were constructed of courses of relatively small stones, while large stone slabs formed a gabled roof, a roofing technique unknown from other Iron Age sites in Israel. The inner dimensions (0.5 m wide; 0.7–0.9 m high) provided adequate crawling space to facilitate cleaning. Massive drains are a well-known feature in Israelite cities. At Timnah they would have been essential, especially during the rainy season, because of the concave surface of the mound created by the massive earthen ramparts of the town's original fortifications. The accumulation of runoff water within the defensive walls during the rainy seasons must have flooded the town's interior on a regular basis. The superbly constructed drain in Area C solved this problem.

Dating the drain's construction posed a difficult problem. During the Persian period, a trench was dug along the line of the drain from topsoil, penetrating almost to the top of the drain itself. For a long time we were sure that the drain

Fig. 5.11. Detailed section of Stratum V (?) drainage channel in Area C.

was constructed during the Persian period, though its elevation corresponds with the bottom of the rectangular structure of the Philistine town. Ultimately, several sections, designed to study this problem, demonstrated that the drain was probably constructed during the Iron Age I, together with the large rectangular building. The Persian period trenching above the drain was probably related to repair and reuse of the drain in the later period.

The accumulated archaeological data indicates that the Philistine town was well-planned and densely populated. The regular raising and repaving of floor levels in open areas of the city suggest an extended occupation and intensive use. There were, however, no specific changes in pottery style during this period. The pottery found at Tel Batash is very similar to that found at nearby sites like Gezer, Beth-Shemesh and Ekron (Strata VI–V) in Iron Age I levels. The assemblage retains local Canaanite traditions with a direct development from the local Late Bronze Age repertoire. However, vessels painted in red and black paint in the Philistine style were the "fine ware" of the period. This style clearly

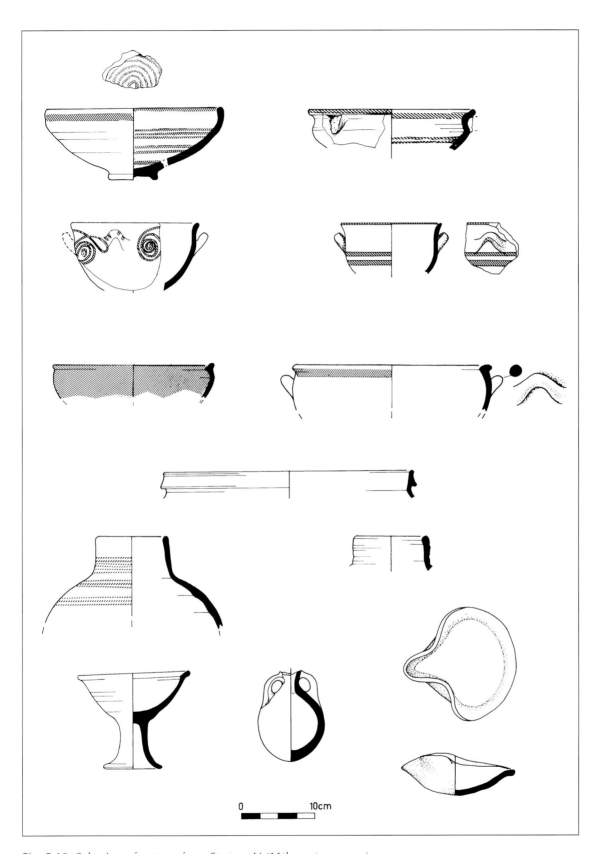

Fig. 5.12. Selection of pottery from Stratum V (11th century B.C.E.).

retained Aegean traditions, though they were mixed with local Canaanite, Egyptian, and Cypriot components.[6] However, the earliest Philistine pottery, discovered exclusively in the major Philistine cities of Ashdod, Ekron, and Ashkelon, is lacking at Timnah. During this first phase, the Philistines produced pottery in a style they brought from their homeland: a local imitation of the Mycenaean IIIC style, known in the Aegean and Cyprus at the beginning of the twelfth century B.C.E.[7] This earliest Philistine pottery, painted in one color only ("monochrome" gray-black or brown) was probably produced only by the first generations of Philistine settlers after their confrontations with Ramesses III. It is the best evidence we have for the earliest settlement of Philistines in the large urban centers of Philistia, known in the Bible as the "five cities of the *Seranim*." The Philistine settlement at Timnah, as well as at many other towns in peripheral Philistia, belonged to a later phase, when the well-known Philistine bichrome style was in vogue.

The demise of Stratum V Timnah can be dated to ca. 1000 B.C.E. The town appears to have come to an end without violence and destruction, perhaps as a result of pressure from the emerging Israelite state of David. It was succeeded by an entirely different city that can be attributed to the reigns of David and Solomon.

Endnotes

1. A. Mazar, "The Iron Age I," in *The Archaeology of Ancient Israel.* (ed. Amnon Ben-Tor; New Haven: Yale University Press, 1992) 258–301.

2. W. F. Albright, *The Excavation of Tell Beit Mirsim, III: The Iron Age* (AASOR 21–22; New Haven, Conn.: American Schools of Oriental Research, 1943) 19–22.

3. M. Dothan, *Ashdod II-III: The Second and Third Seasons of Excavations 1963, 1965; Soundings in 1967* (ᶜAtiqot 9–10; Tel Aviv, 1971) pl. 79:7; M. Shuval, "A Catalogue of Early Iron Stamp Seals from Israel," in O. Keel, M. Shuval, and Ch. Uehlinger, *Studien zu den Stempelsiegeln aus Palästina/Israel* (Fribourg 1990) 112–14, 157.

4. B. Mazar, The Excavations of Tell Qasile, *IEJ* 1 (1951) pl. 36:C.

5. F. M. Cross, "The Evolution of the Proto-Canaanite Alphabet," *BASOR* 134 (1954) 23, fig. 3.

6. Trude Dothan, *The Philistines and their Material Culture* (New Haven: Yale University Press, 1982) 94–218.

7. Trude Dothan, "The Arrival of the Sea Peoples: Cultural Diversity in Early Iron Age Canaan," *AASOR* 49 (1989) 1–22; idem, "Social Dislocation and Cultural Change in the 12th Century B.C., in W. A. Ward and M. S. Joukowsky, *The Crisis Years: The 12th Century B.C.* (Dubuque, 1992) 93–98; Trude and Moshe Dothan, *Peoples of the Sea* (New York: Macmillan Publishing Company, 1992).

6 Timnah During the United Monarchy (Tenth Century B.C.E.)

Historical and Cultural Setting

The Bible is our only historical source for a reconstruction of the events of the United Monarchy. The Biblical narratives, though apparently based on official royal court archives, nonetheless provide only a sketchy portrayal of David's monarchy. The Bible gives the impression that the impetus for acceptance of the monarchy developed during the period of ineffectual judges, whose attempts to consolidate tribal commitment to Israel's common causes failed. Increased territorial pressures on individual tribal borders and resistance to Israelite encroachment by the more integrated ethnic groups highlighted the need for a centralized administration.

During Saul's brief rule, which featured military confrontation on many fronts, the independent tribes reluctantly committed themselves to a rather tenuous political union. With David's accession, a consolidation of tribal unity and military expansion ultimately resulted in an empire extending, according to the biblical narratives, from the Sinai to the Euphrates.

The archaeological evidence for a clarification of the nature of David's monarchy is remarkably poor and hardly consistent with the common conception of Israel's greatest king and his empire. Thriving Canaanite and Philistine towns, such as Megiddo (Stratum VIA) and Tell Qasile (Stratum X) succumbed in fiery conflagrations that may be attributed to David. The Bible, while highlighting his successful militarism, does not attribute any significant building operations to David. His son Solomon was considered the great builder who was responsible for the construction of the royal acropolis in Jerusalem, as well as for a series of fortified cities throughout the kingdom. This seems to suggest that the tenth century B.C.E. was a period in which the Israelites were developing their own distinctive urban culture.[1] The abandonment of many small villages and the development of various towns throughout the country seem to signal the beginning of the new socioeconomic structure of

Fig. 6.1. Map of the traditional allotment of the tribe of Dan, attributed by scholars to Israelite expansion during the United Kingdom.

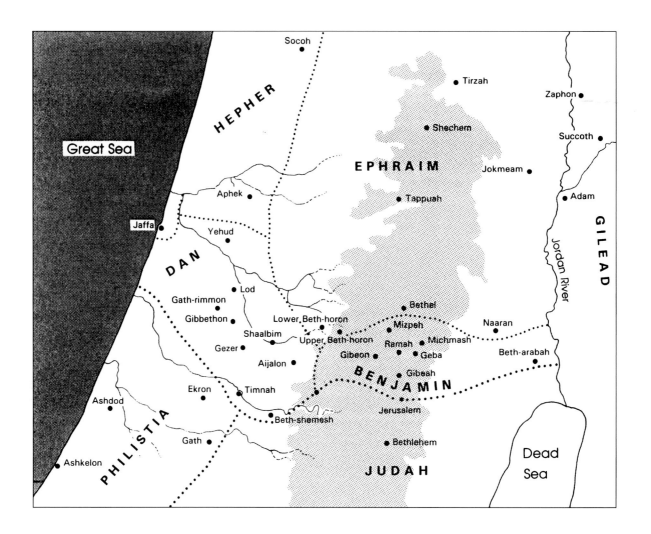

the Israelite monarchy. Occupational strata from this period have been identified at several sites, such as Hazor (Stratum X), Megiddo (Strata VB and IVB–VA), Tel Kinrot, Yoqneam, Tell Qasile (IX–VIII), Beth-Shemesh (Stratum IIa), Gezer (Stratum VIII), Timnah (Stratum IV), Tell Beit Mirsim (Stratum B3), Lachish (Stratum V), Arad, and Beer-sheba in the Negev. At most of these sites, the general impression gained from the architectural remains is of a gradual, tentative urbanization. Thus Lachish, in spite of the fact that it ultimately became a Judean regional capital, had no fortifications during the tenth century B.C.E. and a large portion of its mound remained uninhabited. Clearly, the emergence of Israelite urbanization must be attributed to the latter part of the United Monarchy. Even then, not all urban centers shared equally in its development.

Timnah in the Tenth Century B.C.E.

The destruction of the Philistine town of Timnah (Stratum V) and the emergence of its successor (Stratum IV) may be attributed to Israelite occupation of the town following David's conquest of the region (cf. 1 Sam 8:13–14). David extended his jurisdiction over the northern Shephelah and the region of Jaffa during a western expansion into the coastal plain. The list of Danite cities, which probably reflects David's expansion to this region, mentions Timnah in the form Timnathah (Josh 19:43.).[2] Its location between Eilon and Ekron in the list, following the more easterly cities of Zorah, Eshhtaol, Beth-Shemesh, Shaalbim, and Yitlah, accords well with the identification of Timnah with Tel Batash. The biblical designation of Gezer, together with Megiddo and Hazor, as a royal city (I Kings 9:17–19) may suggest that Timnah, only five miles from Gezer, would have assumed a secondary role in the administrative and economic structure of the region during Solomon's time.

The limited excavation of major architectural units of Stratum IV within the city has unfortunately left the details of this period vague and enigmatic. Excavation in Areas D, E, and H has revealed only a few building remains of Stratum IV. It also appears that the builders of the Stratum III city destroyed much of this earlier city and used stones and other reusable materials from Stratum IV in their building

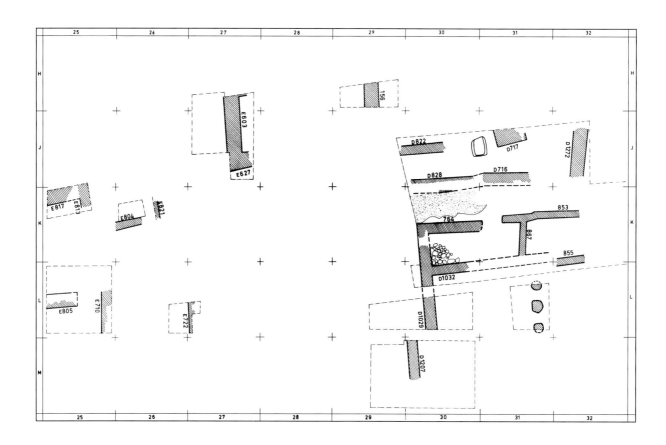

Fig. 6.2. Schematic drawing of Stratum IV architectural remains in Areas D and E.

operations. In most of the excavated areas, architectural remains were in a poor state of preservation and occupational remains of Stratum IV, in general, were scant. The nature of the limited building remains suggests the presence of large open spaces (piazzas, courts, etc.) within the town. No complete building plans could be reconstructed even though some walls were preserved to a height of one or two courses. Some major features of the tenth century city could nevertheless be determined. The town, which was only partly built up, was apparently not densely populated.

A continuous chain of dwellings built along the crest of the mound may have provided a protective perimeter around the tenth century city, with large open piazzas and limited construction in its interior. This is evident from stone foundations built perpendicular to the mound's crest and running below the Strata III-II city wall. In Area D, a narrow lane bordered by poorly-preserved buildings was exposed. The remains were of rather poor, domestic architecture. In one building a line of three pillar bases of large flat stones was preserved. These may have been part of a pillared building of the "four room" type. Farther to the north, a large flat monolithic stone trough was probably part of an industrial complex. It could have been used as the crushing basin of an olive press (and resembles more sophisticated olive oil presses from Stratum II).

Stratigraphic probes in Area E exposed constructional fills containing vast quantities of pottery typical of Stratum IV. These fills were used for levelling areas between foundation walls and beneath the floors of Stratum III. In Area H, fragmentary remains of private dwellings of Stratum IV, similar to those of Area D, were found beneath substantial structures from Stratum III. However, in Areas D and E, Philistine layers of Stratum V were found in several locations directly beneath eighth century B.C.E. (Stratum III) floors, suggesting only partial occupation in those areas during the intervening period.

These remains may reflect an early phase in the growth of a city that failed to achieve an advanced stage of urban development. The lack of evidence for the existence of a city wall was consistent with the situation at other sites in the region, such as Tell Qasile (VIII) and Lachish (V), where a perimeter belt of houses rather than a wall provided a basic line of defense.

The City Gate

Despite the lack of a city wall, entrance to the town was apparently through a city gate built as part of the perimeter belt of houses along the mound's crest. This Stratum IV gate was probably approached by a ramp along the eastern slope of the mound. An L-shaped wall that seems to have been constructed during this phase protected the approach to the gate. The gate passage was flanked by two towers, each approximately measuring 5 × 5 m, constructed with stone foundations against the upper slope. The towers were irregular in shape. The eastern face of the southern tower projected 1.2 m eastward beyond the line of the northern tower, perhaps in order to provide the gate's defenders positioned on the tower with a better view of the approach ramp. The architectural purpose of the stepped recesses in the southwestern corner of this tower remains unclear (unless they served as a type of reinforcement).

Fig. 6.3. Stratum IV *kernos* (libation vessel) spout in the shape of a bull's head.

A single stone door socket in the gate passage, preserved inside the inner corner of the southern tower, provided the pivot for one side of the double door gate. The central gate passage, paved with large flat stones, was 5.5 m wide. The drainage channel beneath the gate complex, which was probably constructed during the earlier Philistine occupation of the town, appears to have continued in use. West of the northern tower, two long east-west brick walls set on stone foundations ran perpendicular to the tower. These parallel walls, 1.0–1.3 m thick with a space of 1.40–1.65 m between them, may have formed a staircase that led to the top of the tower. A square stone pavement between them could have provided the foundation for such stairs. Two stone vats in the corner between these walls and the tower probably served as water troughs for animals. Meager remains of massive walls west of the southern tower were not sufficiently exposed to clarify the plan of this part of the gate complex. The date of construction of this gate is not easy to ascertain, since no clear floor surfaces were found abutting it. We are inclined to attribute it to Stratum IV on the basis of its relative stratigraphic position, the Iron Age pottery found below its foundations, and the typical hand-burnished and red-slipped pottery related to it (though found mainly in fills), which can be no later than the late tenth or early ninth century B.C.E. The gate should therefore be dated to the tenth century B.C.E.

A similar arrangement of two square towers flanking a gate passage was uncovered at nearby Ekron.[3] There, the towers existed as early as the late eleventh century B.C.E. A late eleventh-century gate at Ashdod also had two massive towers.[4] It thus appears that such gates were common in Philistia. The "bent axis" approach to a city gate, with an L-shaped front wall, is known from several Iron Age city gates, such as Dan, Tell el-Far{c}ah (Tirzah) and Beersheba.[5] The citadel gates at Karatepe in Cilicia somewhat resemble our gate in their "bent axis" entrance through an L-shaped wall, leading to a passage between two massive towers.[6]

Finds

Timnah's Stratum IV pottery is characteristic of the Shephelah during the tenth century B.C.E. It included large

Fig. 6.4. Inscription on a bowl rim mentioning (b)n hnn, "son of Hanan." A rare example of a Hebrew inscription of the 10th century B.C.E. (Stratum IV).

kraters with hand-burnished red slip, large two-handled kraters with rounded bodies and narrow necks, and typical cooking pots. Similar pottery at Israelite sites such as Beth-Shemesh (Stratum IIa), Tell Beit Mirsim (Stratum B3), and Lachish (Stratum V) yields further evidence that the occupation of Stratum IV at Timnah lay within the political and economic framework of the Israelite kingdom of David and Solomon. In contrast, a Philistine town such as Ashdod had a distinctly different range of pottery during the tenth century B.C.E.

An important Stratum IV find from Area D was an inscribed pottery sherd. A plain rim of a rounded bowl had been incised before firing with the letters (. . . n/hnn). It should be read: . . .(be)n Hanan (= [belonging to the son of] Hanan). A vertical divider separates the first nun from the name hnn. The letters would fit a tenth century B.C.E. date and are similar to those on the famous Gezer calendar. This is a welcome addition to the very few examples of well-dated tenth century alphabetic inscriptions from Israel. The name Hanan is particularly interesting since it appears as a component of the place name Elon Bethhanan in the second district of Solomon, identified with our region (1 Kgs 4:9).

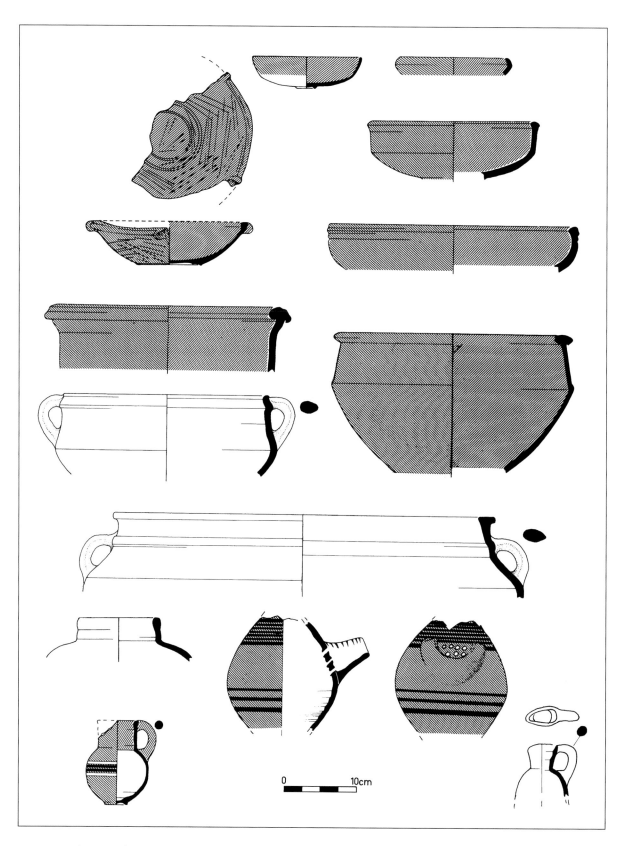

Fig. 6.5. Selection of pottery from Stratum IV (10th century B.C.E.).

"*Elon*" is mentioned before Timnah and Ekron in the list of the cities of Dan (Josh 19:43). It seems likely that the name *Hanan* in our inscription is related to the family of Hanan resident in the region of Elon and Timnah during the tenth century B.C.E.

The destruction of tenth century Timnah (Stratum IV), together with numerous other towns and settlements throughout the country, may be attributed to the invasion by Pharaoh Shishak early in the reign of Rehoboam (923/924 B.C.E.).[7] He passed through the Shephelah on his way to Rubute, Aijalon, Beth-horon, *K-r-t-m* (Kirjath-jearim?), and Gibeon, before challenging Rehoboam at Jerusalem and ultimately striking at strategic positions within Jeroboam's undefended northern kingdom (1 Kgs 14:25–29). The destruction levels at Gezer (Stratum VIII) and Beth-Shemesh (Stratum IIa) also may be attributed to Shishak's campaign. During the ninth century B.C.E. Timnah apparently remained deserted, lying within the buffer zone between the kingdoms of Ekron and Judah.

Endnotes

1. A. Mazar, *Archaeology of the Land of the Bible*, 371–75; G. Barkay, "The Iron Age II–III," in *The Archaeology of Ancient Israel* (ed. Amnon Ben-Tor; New Haven: Yale University Press, 1992) 302–73, esp. 302–15.

2. B. Mazar, "The Cities of the Territory of Dan," *IEJ* 10 (1960) 65–77; Z. Kallai, "The Town Lists of Judah, Simeon, Benjamin and Dan," *VT* 8 (1985) 144–48; R. de Vaux, *The Early History of Israel* (Philadelphia: Westminster, 1978) 777; Z. Kallai, *Historical Geography of the Bible* (Jerusalem: The Magnes Press, 1986); N. Na'aman, "The Inheritance of Dan and the Boundary Systems of the Twelve Tribes," in *Borders and Districts in Biblical Historiography* (Jerusalem: Simor, 1986) 75–117.

3. S. Gitin, "Tel Miqne-Ekron: A Type-Site for the Inner Coastal Plain in the Iron Age II Period," in *Recent Excavations in Israel: Studies in Iron Age Archaeology* (AASOR 49; ed. S. Gitin and W. G. Dever; Winona Lake: Eisenbrauns, 1989) 29, fig. 2.3.

4. M. Dothan and J. Porath, *Ashdod IV: Excavation of Area M* (ᶜAtiqot 15; 1982) Plan V.

5. Z. Herzog, "Settlement and Fortification Planning in the Iron Age," in *The Architecture of Ancient Israel From the Prehistoric to the Persian Periods* (ed. A. Kempinski and R. Reich; Jerusalem: Israel Exploration Society, 1992) 271–74; A. Biran, *Biblical Dan* (Jerusalem, 1994) 235–46; R. de Vaux, "La troisième campagne de fouilles a Tell el-Farᶜah, près Naplouse," *Revue Biblique* 58 (1952) pls. 5–8; Y. Aharoni, "Excavations at Tel Beer-sheba: Preliminary Report on the Fifth and Sixth Seasons, 1973–1974," *Tel Aviv* 2 (1975) 147–48.

6. R. Naumann, *Architektur Kleinasiens* (2nd ed.; Tübingen: Ernest Wasmuth, 1971) 299, Abb. 404–5.

7. B. Mazar, "The Campaign of Pharaoh Shishak to Palestine (*Vetus Testamentum Supplementum* 4; 1957) 57–66; K. A. Kitchen, *The Third Intermediate Period in Egypt* (Warminster: Aris and Phillips, 1973) 293–300, 432–47.

7 Timnah in the Eighth Century B.C.E.

Historical Setting

The collapse of the United Monarchy after Solomon's death and the subsequent feuding of the newly established kingdoms of Rehoboam in the south and Jeroboam in the north significantly increased Israelite vulnerability. Internally, the immediate result was a disruption of the economic and administrative structure that had created the prosperity and opulence of the Solomonic monarchy. The obvious instability and weakened condition of the divided kingdoms immediately enticed the Egyptian pharaoh Shishak to attempt to reestablish Egyptian domination of the lucrative trade routes within the region. The Egyptian attack, however, was no more than a passing episode, though its immediate result was wide-scale destruction in the northern kingdom.

The failure to establish an equitable common border between Israel and Judah was the basic cause of the constant contention and military strife that periodically weakened one or both of the kingdoms, a situation that tempted their neighbors to forays in territorial adventurism. A major threat to Israel came from the Arameans of Damascus early in the ninth century, when Omri and Ahab (882–851 B.C.E.), like David and Solomon of earlier days, achieved considerable wealth and prosperity through strong economic and cultural ties with the Phoenicians and control of the major trade routes, both in Transjordan and the various branches of the Via Maris. As early as the reign of Ahab, the challenge of Assyrian militarism, which would later affect Timnah so seriously, forced a temporary consolidation of the feuding ethnic and geopolitical factions of the region. The success of the Battle of Qarqar (853 B.C.E.), in which Ahab was one of the major allies, in temporarily thwarting Shalmaneser III's imperial march, was soon diminished by a major Aramean-Israelite confrontation in which Ahab was killed. The resulting weakened condition of both sides surely hastened the Assyrians' punitive campaign, which exacted heavy tribute from both Syria and Israel during the reign of Jehu.

During the second half of the ninth century, the region was in a state of revolution and turmoil that culminated in a major confrontation between Judah's Amaziah and Israel's Joash early in the eighth century B.C.E. With Assyrian militarism diverted to other concerns, the diplomacy and cooperation of Judah's Uzziah and Israel's Jeroboam II produced a final period of mutual prosperity during the second quarter of the eighth century. The renewal of Assyrian military expeditions during the second half of the century, however, once again totally disrupted the region's political stability and ultimately led to the collapse of the northern kingdom and the deportation of its population (722/721 B.C.E.).

Timnah at the Time of Sennacherib's Invasion

Annexed to the Assyrian empire, the territory of the northern kingdom of Israel was drastically and irrevocably changed by the Assyrian settlement of foreign "importees." The Judean response under Hezekiah (727–698 B.C.E.), with Egyptian encouragement, was a rebellious consolidation of unenthusiastic allies, such as Philistine Ekron on its western frontier, and an extended period of defensive preparation and organization for revolt. The punitive nature of Sennacherib's campaign in 701 B.C.E. was felt along the entire Levantine coast, though the ultimate Assyrian objective was Jerusalem and the rebellious Hezekiah.[1] After passing through the Phoenician coastal cities, Sennacherib advanced southward and occupied the territories Ashkelon controlled in the region of the Yarkon. His decisive victory at Eltekeh over the token Egyptian army sent to help Hezekiah left the way open for the Assyrian advance into the northern She-phelah. Concerning the conquest of Timnah, Sennacherib's annals reported:

> . . . I besieged Eltekeh and Timnah (Ta-am-na-a), conquered (them) and carried their spoils away. I assaulted Ekron . . ."[2]

The mention of the conquest of Timnah in the context of the war against Ekron seems to emphasize the relationship between the two towns. The nature of the Sennacherib-Hezekiah confrontation, Judah's revolt against Assyria, and Timnah's fate on Hezekiah's western frontier have been

Fig. 7.1. Map: Sennacherib in Philistia and Judah, 701 B.C.E.

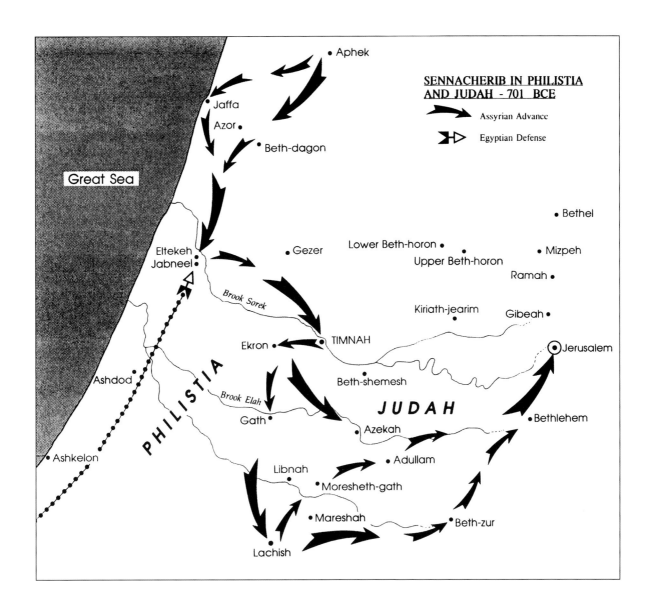

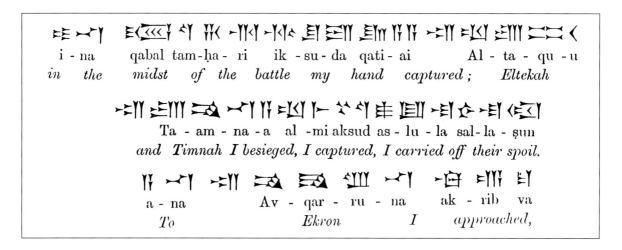

i - na   qabal tam-ḫa- ri   ik -su - da   qati- ai   Al - ta - qu - u

in   *the*   *midst*   *of*   *the*   *battle*   *my*   *hand*   *captured ;*   *Eltekah*

Ta - am - na - a   al -mi aksud as - lu - la   sal-la - ṣun

and   *Timnah I besieged, I captured, I carried off their spoil.*

a - na   Av - qar - ru - na   ak - rib   va

To   *Ekron*   *I*   *approached,*

Fig. 7.2 Part of Sennacherib's annals, mentioning the conquest of Timnah (from George Smith, *History of Sennacherib, Translated from the Cuneiform Inscriptions* [ed. A. H. Sayce; Edinburgh: Williams & Norgate, 1878] 59).

illuminated by the results of our excavations. Clarification came in a most interesting way during the excavation of a building containing an assemblage of *lmlk* jars and destruction debris from Stratum III. After the conquest of Timnah, Ekron probably surrendered peacefully to the Assyrians. Sennacherib then moved to the southern Shephelah, taking Azekah and perhaps Gath. The confrontation with Judah culminated in a decisive siege on Lachish, Judah's second most important city. Sennacherib's annals record the destruction of forty-six towns en route to his siege of Jerusalem. Judah's capital was saved when Sennacherib was forced to withdraw and attend to political problems at home. Thus, the Assyrian invasion of 701 B.C.E. was an important event in the history of the Shephelah in general and of Timnah in particular.

Timnah—Survival as a Frontier Town

Although there is no further mention of Timnah in the Bible until the reign of Ahaz, we suggest that the city was rebuilt by Uzziah during his expansion of Judah's territory at the expense of the Philistines.

> He went out and made war against the Philistines, and broke down the wall of Gath and the wall of Jabneh and the wall of Ashdod; and he built cities in the territory of Ashdod and elsewhere among the Philistines. (2 Chr 26:6)

It is possible that after the destruction of the tenth century city (Stratum IV), Timnah lay in ruins for an extended period until a new town was established. Remains of the new city (Stratum III) indicate major changes in the urban plan. A new gate was erected, and a massive stone wall was built to protect the city. Timnah III architectural remains provide an example of an impressively well-planned and fortified Iron Age city in Judah. The town remained Judean until the time of Ahaz when the Philistines captured Timnah together with other Israelite cities in the Shephelah.

> *And the Philistines had made raids on the cities in the She-phelah and the Negeb of Judah, and had taken Beth-shemesh, Aijalon, Gederoth, Soco with its villages, Timnah with its villages, and Gimzo with its villages; and they set-tled there.* (2 Chr 28:18)

If the Chronicles source adequately reflects the sequence of historical events, Timnah must have become part of the city-state of Ekron at this time. When Hezekiah forced Ek-ron to join his revolt against Assyria, he probably turned

Fig. 7.3. Super-imposed sche-matic plans of Strata I–V in Areas D and E.

Timnah into a Judean garrison town, shortly before it was captured by Sennacherib in 701 B.C.E.

Fortifications for Turbulent Times—Eighth-Seventh Centuries B.C.E. (Strata III–II)

Defensive Walls. Massive defenses of basically the same fortification system protected Timnah during the eighth and seventh centuries B.C.E. The defenses of the eighth century remained intact and continued in use with only minimal changes during the seventh century, despite Sennacherib's conquest of the town in 701 B.C.E.

The Iron Age city wall was exposed along 75 m of the northern crest of the mound (Strata III–II in Areas D, E, and F). The massive eighth-century stone wall (ca. 3 m wide) was

Fig. 7.4. Schematic plan of Stratum III structures in Areas D and E (8th century B.C.E.).

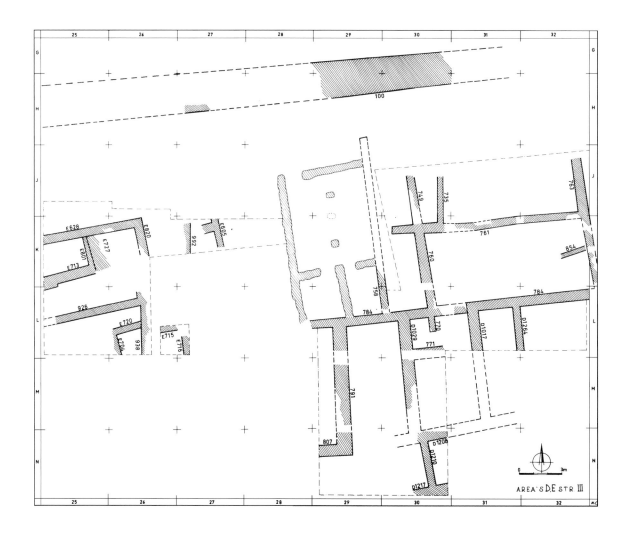

reinforced during the seventh century on its inner side with an additional meter or more of solid stone facing.

A lower stone wall provided a first line of defense near the base of the slope. This outer wall, preserved to a height of 1.6 m, was constructed of large boulders comparable to a terrace wall (with no inner face). Its exterior, however, gave the appearance of a massive fortification wall. Its primary purpose was apparently to serve as an effective first line of defense against the battering ram and other siege operations.

In the eighth century, the slope between the two walls consisted of an earthen glacis of compacted layers of alluvial soil and river pebbles. During the seventh century this glacis was resurfaced with courses of stone, a feature which partly survived near the crest of the slope below the upper defensive wall. Similar fortification systems are known to have existed in other Judean cities. Lachish, for example, was surrounded by a double wall similar to the Timnah system, and examples of earthen glacis have been found at Beersheba and other sites.[3]

Fig. 7.5. General view of Area D, showing remains of storage building of Stratum III superimposed by a 7th century B.C.E. building of Stratum II. The Iron Age II city wall is seen along the northern crest of the mound (looking northwest).

South of the inner gate structure, a more massive city wall was uncovered. The initial wall was only 2 m wide, and abutted the inner gate structure of Stratum III opposite its central chamber. In Phase IIIA reinforcement on its inner face produced a 3.1-m-thick wall. Beyond a 2.2-m space, a parallel inner wall, 1.70–1.95 m wide, probably constructed during this phase (or as early as Phase IIIB) created a 7-m-wide double wall system. This structure was exposed for 15 m between the inner gate of Stratum III and a large building in Area H. The construction of the inner wall as a continuation of the inner piers of the Stratum III gate structure indicates the existence of an integrated strategic architectural plan for the entire area. The effectiveness of this massive fortification system was enhanced by the revetment wall on the slope of the mound.

The City Gates. The Iron Age II city gate (Strata III-II) was a monumental architectural complex on the eastern slope of the mound, with an approach ramp from the north. The well-preserved ramp, 4 m wide, was protected by a mas-

Fig. 7.6. General view of Strata III–II gate (view to the north).

sive 2.8-m-wide outer retaining wall built of large unworked stones. Another retaining wall supported the slope of the mound above the ramp. The gate complex consisted of two distinct defensive units: a massive outer gate built against the eastern slope of the mound and an inner gate structure on the mound's crest. The gate structures had suffered from severe erosion and were poorly preserved, with only foundation courses preserved directly below surface soil. Though the pavement of the gate passage was partly preserved, the floors of the adjoining gate chambers were totally eroded. The eastern portion of the inner gate near the crest of the mound also was severely damaged by erosion.

Study of the architectural sequence of these gates was complicated by the complex history of repair and reuse of

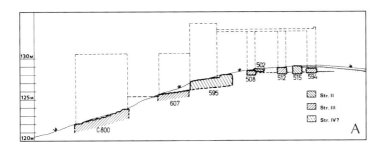

Fig. 7.7. Plans and section of Strata IV, III, and II city gates.
A: East-west section through the northern part of the gate structures.
B: Plan of Stratum III gate including Towers 543, 595 of Stratum IV. Walls 631 and 608 were founded in Stratum IV.
C: Plan of the gate in Stratum II.

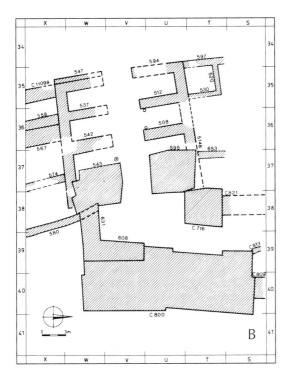

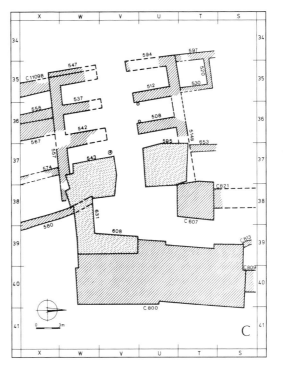

the Stratum III foundations and walls by the builders of Stratum II. Few finds could be attributed with certainty to a specific context. Their dating and stratigraphic attribution were based on their relationship to the city wall and to the buildings found above and beneath them. Some of the basic features of the gate plans appear in the schematic plans.

The outer gate complex consisted of a massive 8 × 21 m bastion, with a perpendicular wall at its southern end that connected it to the inner gate. At its northern end, a counter tower (5 × 5 m) protected a 3.5-m-wide entrance to the city. The foundation courses of the bastion were built of massive unworked boulders, some approaching 1.5 m in diameter. A 2.5-m-deep probe at the northeastern corner of the bastion exposed four courses of stones below the present alluvial plain at the base of the tell. The walls of the bastion had been built with a series of 0.5 m offsets. Similar offsets are characteristic of other Iron Age II fortifications in Judah and Israel.

Fig. 7.8. Stone foundation of massive outer gate tower (Stratum III), looking northwest.

The smaller tower of the outer gate was attached to the northern tower of the Stratum IV gate. Similarly, the larger bastion was in fact an enlargement of the L-shaped wall of the Stratum IV gate. The doors of the outer gate were placed where the passage between the large bastion and the smaller tower narrowed to 2.9 m. The massive bastion may have risen to a height of 7–8 m and controlled the bent-axis passage into the inner gate. The passage roadbed was badly eroded, with only a few fragments of its surface preserved.

The plan of the inner gate, common in the Iron Age II, included a central passage flanked by a series of guardrooms formed by piers constructed at right angles to the passage. The two towers of the Stratum IV gate must have been in ruins when part of the inner gate of Stratum III was built over

Fig. 7.9. Artist's conception of Timnah's massive gate complex.

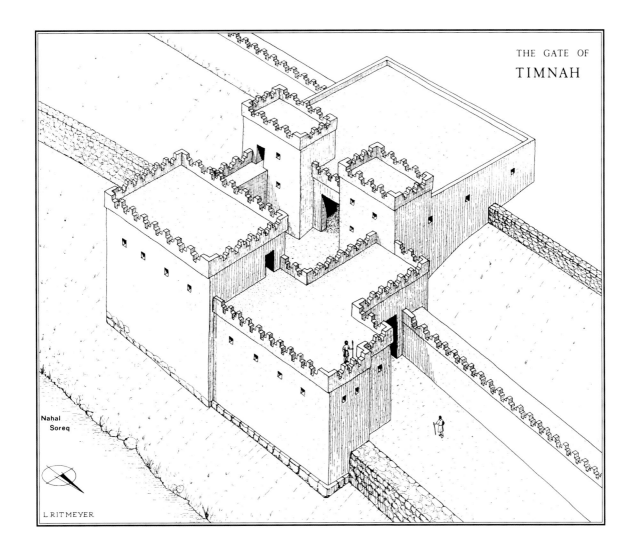

THE GATE OF
TIMNAH

Nahal
Soreq

L RITMEYER

them. The width of the inner gate, enclosed by two outer east-west walls (1.25 m wide), is 16.7 m. Its length could only be estimated since its eastern end was completely eroded. Four guardrooms of the Stratum III inner gate were preserved. Their length was 4.8 m, while their width varied from 2.5 to 2.9 m. While the piers north of the gate passage are well preserved, those on the south side had been partly destroyed during the Persian period repair of the drainage channel. In spite of destructive erosion along the mound's crest, another pair of chambers could have existed at the eastern end of the inner gate. If this reconstruction is correct, the inner gate had three pairs of guardrooms and could be considered a "six-chambered" gate, a type known at a number of Iron Age II sites in Israel.[4] At Megiddo, Hazor, and Gezer, this plan has been dated to the Solomonic era. At Lachish and perhaps at Ashdod it is slightly later. At Tel Miqne (Ekron) and Tel ꜥIra in the northern Negev, gates of this type were constructed during the eighth and seventh centuries B.C.E. The general plan of the city gate, with a protected approach ramp, outer gate with massive bastion and an inner six-chambered gate, in many respects resembles the city gate of Lachish in the eighth century B.C.E. The Lachish gate was in use during Strata IV–III and was destroyed by Sennacherib in 701 B.C.E. A similar (though smaller) gate was constructed in Lachish Stratum IV, at the entrance to the royal enclosure of Stratum III.[5] The common influence that produced these similarities supports the hypothesis that Timnah Stratum III was built as a Judean town. Similarities in architectural design also exist between the Timnah bastion and the large "Warren's Tower" in the Ophel of Jerusalem (named after its discoverer, Charles Warren), which also may have served as an outer defense for a gate.[6]

The roadbed of the 4-m-wide inner gate passage consisted of beaten earth laid over an earlier cobblestone surface. At the entrance to one of the gate chambers the lower part of a storage jar was found embedded in the floor. This *lmlk*-type jar was similar to those found in a Stratum III building in Area D.

The formidable outer gate of Stratum III does not seem to have been damaged during Sennacherib's conquest of Timnah, since it continued in use throughout the seventh century B.C.E. (Stratum II) without any architectural change.

The inner gate, however, was reconstructed and shortened in Stratum II. Only one pair of guardrooms survived, though there was adequate space for another pair in the eastern eroded part of the gate complex. It thus seems to have been a "four-chambered" gate.

The Eighth Century B.C.E. City (Stratum III)

Timnah of the eighth century B.C.E. (Stratum III) appears to have been a well-planned town, with massive public buildings, residential quarters and barracks.

Stratum III Public Buildings in Area H. Excavation of Area H, begun in 1985, continued into the final season (1989) to provide extensive exposure of the area south of the city gate. The total area excavated is 425 sq m, most of which reached Stratum III and IV levels. Iron Age II remains in this area were badly eroded. The entire accumulation of Stratum III–II is less than 1 m in depth. The walls were usually preserved as a single course of stones, and the Stratum II remains are found near topsoil.

To clarify the relationship of the public buildings in Area H to the inner gate structure in Area C, Area H was extended northward to form a continuous area with Area C. Eventually, a strip 50 m long and almost 15 m wide was excavated from the southern edge of the inner gate structure in Area C to the southern end of Area H. This wide-scale exposure permitted a comprehensive study of the rather complicated architectural history of this area in Strata III and II.

The private dwellings of Stratum IV uncovered in this area were replaced in Stratum III by a large public building which may have been incorporated in the fortifications of the city. Two phases of construction in Stratum III have been designated IIIB and IIIA.

The 7-m-wide double wall system that was probably part of the city wall ran across the northern part of the area. This city wall abuts a monumental building 15.5 m south of the gate structure, erected near the crest of the mound.[12] The eastern side of this building was eroded away, and only its western foundations were preserved. These stone foundations are mostly 1.4 m wide, though one wall is more than 2 m wide. Like the city wall to the north, the walls of this building are preserved to a height of one course and are leveled at the top as if to serve as a socle for a mudbrick superstructure. The northern part of this building was built as a continuation of the double-walled system described above, and both elements were probably planned together. This part includes two rooms, about 3.2–3.4 m wide. The western room is almost square. The length of the eastern one was at least 3.6 m, though its eastern end was completely eroded. These rooms are known only in outline; their interiors were not excavated. The two rooms are bounded on the south by a 2-m-wide east-west wall that was preserved for a length of 14.5 m. South of this wall, two parallel 2-m-wide walls, 3 m apart, continue the line of the double-walled system near the gate structure. The two walls are bounded on the south by a massive wall, which is probably the outer wall of the entire complex. Inside, an inner partition wall creates two rooms: an elongated hall (3.0 × 6.5 m inner dimensions) and a smaller chamber (1.85 × 3.0 m). The excavated rooms of this building probably form

Fig. 7.10. Plan of buildings of Stratum III in Area H (8th century B.C.E.).

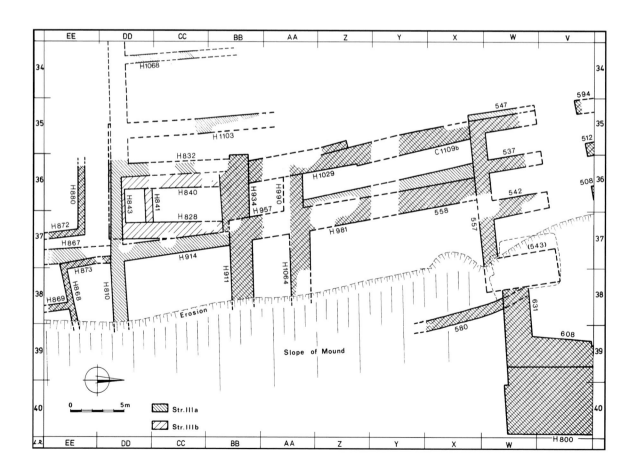

only a small part of the entire complex: fragmentary remains suggest that it had additional rooms farther to the west, and the eastern wing of the building was eroded away. It may be conjectured that this side was solidly built and served as part of the fortification system of the city.

The building, constructed in Phase IIIB, was restored in Phase IIIA. Some of its rooms had been damaged. The building of Phase IIIA also had a slightly different plan: the north-south walls of the main hall were built running diagonally to the line of the original walls and the inner partition was removed. The new hall now had inner dimensions of 5.8 × 10 m.

The large building of Stratum III in Area H was designed together with the gate and the double-walled system that connected the two as part of a comprehensive town plan. An area of at least 1200 sq m (including the outer and inner gates) had been architecturally integrated here as part of the fortifications and administrative complex. It may be conjectured that this large building in Area H had been the

Fig. 7.11. The central part of Area H (Strata III–II), looking east.

Fig. 7.12. Typical *lmlk* storage jars and scoops.

town's main administrative center and perhaps the governor's headquarters. Private dwellings to the south of this large building reflect two similar structural phases in their relatively thin walls. In this area, the eastern wall of the town appears to have been located beyond the erosion line. The structural modifications of the Phase IIIB–A transition yield evidence of a major event in the eighth century B.C.E., possibly the earthquake during Uzziah's reign (Amos 1:1) or the conquest by the Philistines during the reign of Ahaz (2 Chr 28:18). The entire architectural complex in Area H was probably destroyed by Sennacherib and the area assumed a different character during the seventh century (Stratum II).

The Judean Stronghold at Timnah

In the eastern part of Area D, near the highest point of the mound, we uncovered a large building of Stratum III that went out of use in Stratum II. This building is located south of the city wall. It had been divided into at least three large rooms with rather thin stone wall construction. One of these, 9.9 m long, was a large hall, with a stone pavement covered by a thick layer of lime. The presumed northern wall of this room was probably destroyed by the later construction of a massive building in Stratum II. The western part of the building consisted of four smaller rooms, some with thick lime floors. It appears that this was a storehouse for food, and that the quality of floor construction was a possible precaution against insects, rodents, etc. On the floor of this hall we found scattered fragments of many pottery storage jars of the well-known Judean *lmlk*-type (= '*belonging to the king*'), with the royal Judean seal impressions on some handles (Type 484, according to Tufnell's typology at Lachish).[7] Concentrations of these sherds were found beneath a Stratum II stone floor.

A tedious and meticulous restoration process yielded fourteen complete jars; restoration of six others was almost complete; and fragments of another twenty jars have been identified. Thus, at least 30–40 jars were stored in this building. All the jars were produced using a similar technique. The dark brown clay with many small lime inclusions had been fired at a high temperature, giving the vessels a gray core and a "metallic" ring. Neutron activation analysis

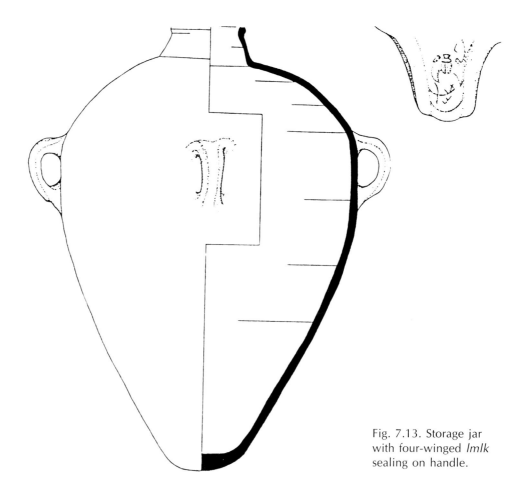

Fig. 7.13. Storage jar with four-winged *lmlk* sealing on handle.

carried out in the archaeometry laboratory of the Institute of Archaeology of The Hebrew University conclusively demonstrated that all the jars had been made with clay from the same source as other *lmlk* jars analyzed from other sites throughout Judah.[8] The exact profile and capacity of the jars varied (39–56 liters).

The handles of these Judean *lmlk* jars had been stamped with a royal seal while still in the pottery workshop. More than one thousand such seal impressions have been recovered throughout Judah, all bearing the *lmlk* imprint (= "belonging to the king") and one of four place names: *Hebron, Sochoh, Ziph,* and *Mamshat.* Each inscription is accompanied by an emblem: either a four-winged scarab or a two-winged symbol. However, in only a few cases have complete jars with the seal impressions been found, and in even fewer cases has a whole assemblage of such jars been found in a single structure. The assemblage from this building is thus most important for the study of this interesting subject. Of the fourteen completely restored jars, only two had stamped handles. One of these has an illegible four-winged sealing on one handle, while the other jar has all four handles sealed in a unique manner: instead of using a seal, the potter produced the seal impressions with another handle, which had previously been sealed with a four-winged seal reading *lmlk skh* ('belonging to the king, Sochoh'). Thus, the seal impressions on our jar were illegible negatives of an original seal impression.

Six more *lmlk* seal impressions were found in this building on handles of jars that were not restorable. Two of these are illegible four-winged seal impressions, and four others are two-winged *lmlk* seal impressions: three of these impressions were legible, with the names of the cities *Ziph* and *Mamshat*. In addition, a personal seal impression, *lṣfn abmᶜṣ* (= 'belonging to Ṣafan son of Abimaᶜaṣ') was found in the same room. An identical seal impression was found in the Jewish Quarter excavations in Jerusalem near the massive Iron Age city wall, together with *lmlk* seal impressions of both four-winged and two-winged types.[9] Another identical seal impression was found at Tel Azekah in the Shephelah. The name "Ṣafan" also appears on other seals and seal impressions from Judah and on a jug from Jerusalem.[10] Seal impressions from Lachish with the names *Ṣafan (son of) Azaryahuᵓ* (three such impressions were found there) and *Hoshᶜa (son of) Ṣafan*, possibly stamped on *lmlk* jar handles, are comparable. May we assume that this *Ṣafan* was one and the same man, a high official of Hezekiah's time? These and other personal seal impressions appearing together with *lmlk* seal impressions probably record the names of officials responsible for the production of the jars, or to the administration related to their production.

The evidence from Timnah corresponds well with discoveries at Lachish, where four-winged and two-winged stamps were found on restorable jars in Stratum III storehouses destroyed in the 701 B.C.E. Assyrian conquest.[11] There is therefore no chronological distinction between the two types of seals, as was once supposed.

The contents of this building have provided important insights into the use of the *lmlk* jars. The ratio of sealed to

Fig. 7.14. Private sealing on *lmlk* jar reading: *lṣfn abmᶜṣ* 'belonging to Ṣafan (son of) Abimaᶜaṣ'.

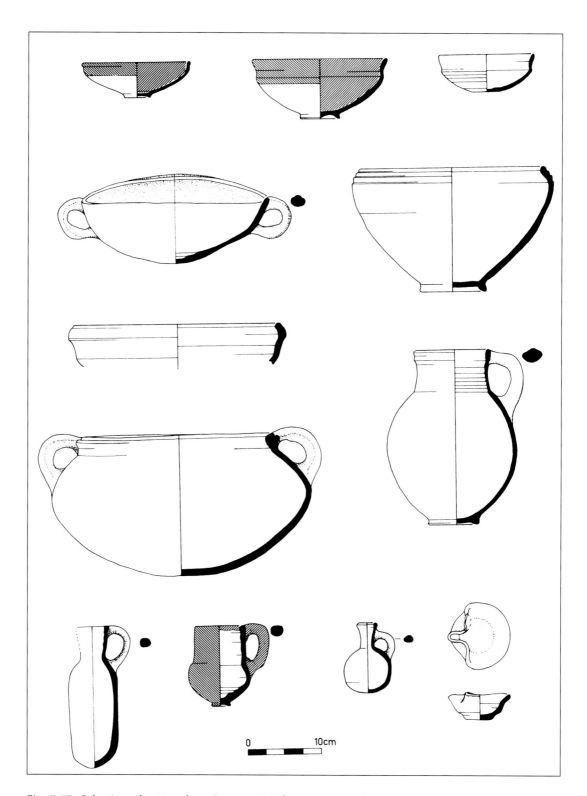

Fig. 7.15. Selection of pottery from Stratum III (8th century B.C.E.).

unsealed jars is similar to that found at Lachish. At both sites only a few of the jars of this type were sealed, and most in the assemblage remained unsealed. Perhaps a selection of jars from each production lot was sealed. Even more rare was the use of the personal seal. The homogeneity of the production and of the clay, the probable mass production reflected in the manufacturing procedures, and the manner in which the seals were impressed, reinforce the conclusion that these jars were prepared hastily, presumably shortly before Sennacherib's invasion, as part of Hezekiah's preparations for the war with Assyria.

The *lmlk* jars presumably were brought to this public building in the northeast quadrant of Timnah during Hezekiah's frantic defensive preparations for Sennacherib's assault. Hezekiah's domination of Ekron before 701 B.C.E. would have included control of Timnah, whether it was considered a secondary town within the city-state of Ekron or actually was a Judean town at the time. Thus the *lmlk* jars were used for the transport of food supplies for the Judean garrison stationed at Timnah. Such a scenario is consistent with the recovery of large numbers of *lmlk* jars at other sites destroyed by Sennacherib. The jars presumably produced during the years immediately before 701 B.C.E. were used for the collection and storage of taxes-in-kind (grain, wine, oil, etc.), possibly the result of special levies intended to ensure an emergency food supply for the war effort. Ultimately, however, the jars recovered at Timnah served as shipment and distribution containers for foodstuffs for Hezekiah's forces, in anticipation of the imminent Assyrian assault.

Dwellings and other Building Remains of Stratum III. Very little is known about the dwellings in the eighth century Stratum III at Timnah. Well-preserved dwellings and industrial installations of Stratum II of the seventh century B.C.E. were exposed in Areas D, E, and F. However, we rarely excavated below their floors. The "Oil Press Building" in Area E may have existed with a slightly different plan as early as Stratum III, and Building 743 in Area D, a Stratum II dwelling, also may have had an earlier history in Stratum III (see below). The details of its earlier configuration are unknown, however. A Stratum II street along the northern city wall probably existed as early as Stratum III; it was paved with cobblestones and had a drainage channel in its center.

The basic character of the Iron Age II town apparently was established in Stratum III on the basis of a carefully devised town plan.

Drastic structural changes, however, did occur in the western part of Area E during the transition between Strata III and II. The spaces between three parallel walls found in this part of the site consisted of 1 m of constructional fill, containing vast quantities of red-slipped and hand-burnished pottery, typical of Stratum IV. The builders of Stratum III apparently leveled this area in preparation for the building of a large structure. Tenth-century (Stratum IV) buildings were destroyed during this operation, their stones saved and re-used in the new structures, and the debris leveled as foundational fill.

Because of the fragmentary nature of the architectural remains, the nature and purpose of the new buildings in this area remain unclear. However, restorable pottery from a floor within this restricted area yielded one of the best Stratum III assemblages.

Female Figurine Molds. An exceptional find from eighth-century Timnah consisted of three clay molds for casting ceramic figurines, recovered from a Stratum III floor in Area E. They were found just above the constructional fill of Stratum III, sealed by Stratum II walls and floors in Square K26, and are securely dated to the late eighth century B.C.E. The molds were formed by pressing lumps of clay onto master originals. Even the finger prints of the potter have been preserved on the body of the molds. Two molds of nude standing female figurines are complete. The head of a female figurine, cast from the upper part of a third (broken) mold, exhibits the finest workmanship of the three. It portrays a beautiful, fleshy female face, with a necklace and coiffure resembling Phoenician depictions of women. Its detailed workmanship suggests an ivory original of a fully sculptured or high-relief female figure. Although the original was sculptured in the round, the artisan, in preparing the mold, found it impossible to capture more than the frontal features (including the front parts of the coiffure).

The two complete molds exhibit distinctive elements. One produced a figurine of a nude female supporting her breasts with her hands, standing on a small square pedestal. (This "pedestal" probably served as a square plug that could be

inserted into an appropriate socket to hold the figurine up-right.) The nose of the figure is somewhat distorted, possibly the result of the artisan's careless removal of the modeling clay from the "master" statuette. In profile, however, the delicate details of this figure's other facial features are clearly evident.

The second complete mold produced a standing nude figure with her arms at her sides. The head of the figure was disproportionately large for its slender body and its hands were unusually long. The large eyes and the "archaic" smile suggest the influence of Cypriot or Phoenician art.

The artistic style of the figures and the details of their physiognomy are exceptional among the clay figurines found in Iron Age Palestine. No similar works of art are known in Judah, though a few clay heads in a similar style have been found in Philistia (particularly at Tel Sera[c]). The molds may

Fig. 7.16. Three female figurines cast from clay molds found in Area E (Stratum III).

represent a local artistic style that flourished in Philistia during the eighth century B.C.E. However, they also could have been made from imported originals, perhaps from Phoenicia.

The End of Stratum III. The city was partly destroyed during the Assyrian conquest in 701 B.C.E. The inner gate in Area C, the public building in Area H, and the *lmlk* jar building in Area D were all destroyed during this struggle. Other structures continued in use during the next century with only minor, if any, modifications to the town plan.

Endnotes

1. B. Mazar, "The Campaign of Sennacherib in Judea," *Eretz-Israel* 2 (1953) 170–75 (Hebrew); N. Na'aman, "Sennacherib's Campaign in Judah and the Date of the *lmlk* Stamps," *VT* 29 (1979) 62–86.

2. *ANET*, 287–88.

3. Z. Herzog, in *The Architecture of Ancient Israel* (ed. A. Kempinski and R. Reich; Jerusalem: Israel Exploration Society, 1992) 265–71; Z. Herzog, in Y. Aharoni, *Beer-sheba I: Excavations at Tel Beer-sheba 1969–1971 Seasons* (Publications of the Institute of Archaeology 2; Tel Aviv: Institute of Archaeology, University of Tel Aviv, 1973) 10, 11; D. Ussishkin, "Excavations at Tell Lachish, Preliminary Report," *Tel Aviv* 10 (1983) 142–43; J. Seger, "Investigation at Tel Halif, Israel 1976–1980," *BASOR* 252 (1983) 11–15.

4. This was first suggested by Baruch Brandl, the field supervisor of Area C. See also D. Ussishkin, "Notes on Megiddo, Gezer, Ashdod, and Tel Batash in the Tenth to Ninth Centuries B.C.," *BASOR* 277–278 (1990) 71–91. His observation that the Tel Batash gate was of six-chambered type is reasonable, but his observations concerning the substructure of this gate are unacceptable.

5. D. Ussishkin, "Excavations at Tell Lachish," 147–51.

6. E. Mazar and B. Mazar, *Excavations in the South of the Temple Mount* (Qedem 29; Jerusalem, 1989) Plans 2, 7. Compare O. Tufnell, *Lachish III: The Iron Age* (London, 1953) 316, pl. 95.

7. In preliminary notes, we attributed the foundation of the large building in Area H to Stratum IV. During the 1988 season it became increasingly clear that the large building in Area H had been founded in Stratum III.

8. H. Mommsen, I. Perlman, and J. Yellin, "The Provenience of the LMLK Jars," *IEJ* 34 (1984) 89–113.

9. N. Avigad, "Excavations in the Jewish Quarter, Jerusalem," *IEJ* 20 (1970) 129–40 (esp. p. 131).

10. D. Diringer, "On Ancient Hebrew Inscriptions Discovered at Tell ed-Duweir (Lachish) I, II," *PEQ* 74 (1941) 38–40, 55; R. Hestrin and M. Dayagi-Mendels, *Inscribed Seals of the First Temple Period* (Israel Museum Catalogue; Jerusalem: Israel Museum and Department of Antiquities, 1979) nos. 23, 90; J. Prignaud, "Scribes et graveurs à Jerusalem, vers 700 av. J-C." in *Archaeology in the Levant: Essays for Kathleen Kenyon* (ed. P. R. S. Moorey and P. J. Parr. Warminster: Aris and Phillips, 1978) 136.

11. D. Ussishkin, "The Destruction of Lachish by Sennacherib and the Dating of the Royal Judean Storage Jars," *Tel Aviv* 4 (1977) 28–60; idem, "Royal Judean Storage Jars and Private Seal Impressions," *BASOR* 223 (1976) 1–13; idem, *The Conquest of Lachish by Sennacherib* (Tel Aviv, 1982).

8 Timnah during the Seventh Century B.C.E.

Historical Setting

During the seventh century, the economic and political stability of Assyrian administration throughout the Levant fostered vibrant regional economies, in spite of oppressive tribute imposed on regional urban centers. This relative prosperity and the development of distinctive local cultures under the aegis of the Assyrian empire is evident at excavations throughout Israel and Transjordan. This period of "Pax Assyriaca" fostered local industries and extensive international trade relations.[1] Assyrian finds at sites such as Tel Sera^c, Tell Jemmeh, and Tell Abu Salima on the southern coastal plain and in northern Sinai clearly suggest an Assyrian strategy of maintaining strong control over southern Palestine, as the gateway to domination of Egypt.[2] Gezer was an Assyrian administrative and military stronghold in this region. Ekron grew during this time from 10 to 50 acres and as an important city-state became a major center for olive oil production.[3]

When the Assyrian imperial hold on Palestine ultimately weakened and almost disappeared after 630 B.C.E., Egypt once again appeared on the stage and tried to gain control of the coastal plain of Palestine. With the fall of Nineveh in

612 B.C.E. and the collapse of the Assyrian Empire, the Egyptians attempted intervention in Mesopotamian affairs to thwart the threat of Babylon's rise to power. This event became the backdrop for the death of Josiah at Megiddo, where he had confronted Pharaoh Necho II of the Twenty-sixth Dynasty, who was intent on helping the Assyrians. Soon, however, the Babylonians, who claimed territorial rights over the far-flung Assyrian provinces, appeared in the coastal plain of Palestine. Nebuchadnezzar's campaigns in Philistia occurred between 605 and 601 B.C.E. and brought fiery destruction to major cities like Ekron and Ashkelon. Judah did not escape and Jerusalem ultimately fell in 586 B.C.E.

Timnah During the Seventh Century B.C.E. (Stratum II)

Fig. 8.1 Map: The Expansion of the Assyrian Empire.

Timnah was soon restored following its partial destruction during Sennacherib's conquest in 701 B.C.E. Much of its

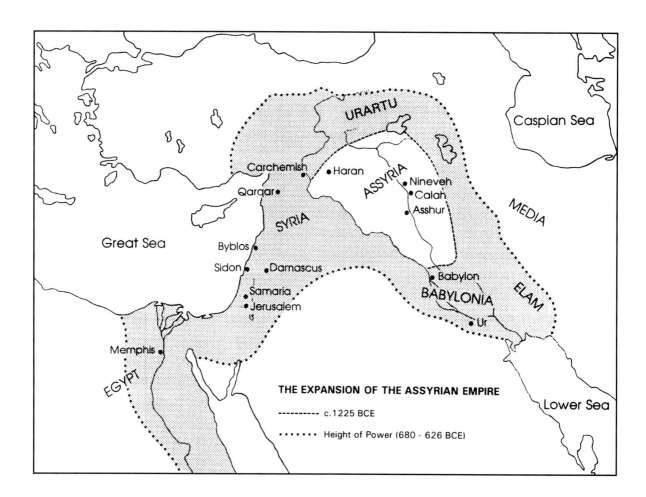

THE EXPANSION OF THE ASSYRIAN EMPIRE

--------- c.1225 BCE

•••••• Height of Power (680 - 626 BCE)

earlier eighth-century urban plan was retained throughout the seventh century (Stratum II). This extensive final occupational stratum at Timnah represents a well-planned, prosperous town with its own distinctive material culture. Its clearest affinities are to Ekron, its nearest neighbor to the west. The vitality of local industries suggests that Timnah thrived under the economic and political stability imposed by Assyrian domination throughout most of the Levant. One of the major questions regarding this period is whether seventh-century Timnah was a Judean town or whether it was part of the city-state of Ekron. We will return to this question later.

The final destruction of Timnah must have taken place during the Babylonian invasions, sometime between 605 and 601, and probably in 603 B.C.E. It signalled the demise of the city. Some scanty evidence of temporary squatters on the site following this massive destruction hardly qualifies as a subsequent reoccupation.

Architectural Remains

The continuation of the basic features of Timnah's city plan into the seventh century (Stratum II) clearly indicates that the Assyrians did not completely destroy the town in 701 B.C.E. The excavation exposed large areas of this city along most of the eastern and northern half of the mound's crest (Areas C, D, E, F, and H), where occupational strata tended to slope toward the central depression created by the original Middle Bronze Age earthen ramparts. While some of the older eighth-century buildings continued in use without any radical change, other Stratum III buildings destroyed by Sennacherib were replaced with new buildings in the seventh century B.C.E.

In Area D, the eighth century *lmlk* jars building (Building 737) of Stratum III was replaced in Stratum II by a large public building. Stratum III buildings were destroyed and replaced by new buildings in the seventh century in the western part of Area E as well. However, private dwellings in Areas D and E (Buildings 743 and 950, the "Oil Press Building") seem to have originated in the eighth century and were reconstructed and modified in Stratum II. In Area H, the public structures of the eighth century were replaced by an

Fig. 8.2. General view of Iron Age II buildings in Areas D and E (view to east). Left: city wall of Strata III–II.

entirely new architectural complex in Stratum II. The fortifications and general street layout of the eighth-century town were retained during the seventh century; thus, the street along the northern city wall continued to exist through the seventh century B.C.E.

Fortifications

The stone foundation courses of the fortification system of the Stratum II town are exposed along most of the mound's crest. The solid city wall that still protrudes above topsoil in many places along the crest was reinforced on the inside in Areas D and E, increasing its width to about 4 m. Its inner face was well preserved to a height of three courses (1 m), though the outer face of the wall tilted outward and was poorly preserved. Several courses of a stone glacis remained intact, extending for 2 m down the slope below the wall. The rest of the glacis had eroded away. This protective glacis was clearly intended to prevent or at least to limit erosion of the wall foundations (see fig. 2.3).

The outer (or lower) city wall along the lower part of the slope apparently continued in use without change. A thick layer of fallen stones and debris extending beyond it for twelve meters on the lower slope, toward the outer edge of the supposed Middle Bronze moat, probably contains the collapsed remnants of the Iron Age city walls.

At the base of the eastern slope, the outer gate with its monumental bastion continued in use without change in Stratum II. The inner gate, however, was rebuilt on the shorter four-chambered plan. Thick layers of small brook pebbles were used to pave the gate passage and a large piazza within the inner gate that may have been the open air commercial and social center for the town. The thick pebble pavement of the piazza extended over the western extensions of the Stratum III gate, which went out of use during the seventh century. This "shortening" of the city gate plan in the Stratum III–II transition is consistent with a general architectural development throughout the country. Thus, at Megiddo, a four-chambered gate was replaced by a two-chambered gate, probably in the Strata IV–III transition.[4]

Fig. 8.3. Iron Age II city wall with attached gutter and street levels (Area D).

The Northern Residential Quarter

A Public Structure in Area D. A large public building in Area D was constructed in Stratum II over the ruins of the Stratum III *lmlk* jars building. Two long walls of this complex were excavated, each 1.1 m wide and constructed of large unworked stones. The wide foundation trench of the northern wall (16.4 m long) cut through the massive floors of the Stratum III building and yielded fragments of *lmlk* jars in its fill. The western wall of the building (14 m exposed) was built upon the eastern wall of a Stratum III dwelling and also served as the eastern wall of Building 743, an adjoining dwelling on the west.

The complete plan of the large square public building to which these massive walls belonged is unknown. Two partition walls in its eastern portion had a massive stone pavement between them. Two large stone gutters (probably modified monolithic pillars in secondary use) were incorporated into its northern wall. Beyond the wall, a drainage channel ran from the eastern gutter across the street and westward along the base of the northern city wall. Such gutters, unknown in other Iron Age buildings, may have been

Fig. 8.4. Building complex of Iron Age II along northern city wall, Area D (looking northeast).

essential for some type of industrial activity inside the building. Very few pottery sherds or other finds could be attributed to this structure, since most of the floors were eroded away. Located on the highest point of the mound, this building could have been an administrative center or a citadel for the town.

Residential Dwellings. Extensive excavation of four complete houses and portions of other buildings (in Areas D, E, and F) clarified the principles of urban planning during the seventh century B.C.E. in the northern part of the town. A 3.5-m-wide street along the interior of the northern city wall was exposed at intervals along 75 meters. It had been constructed during the eighth century and repaved at least twice with beaten earth during the seventh century. A row of buildings bordered the southern side of this street.

Fig. 8.5. Schematic plan of structures in Areas D and E (Stratum II).

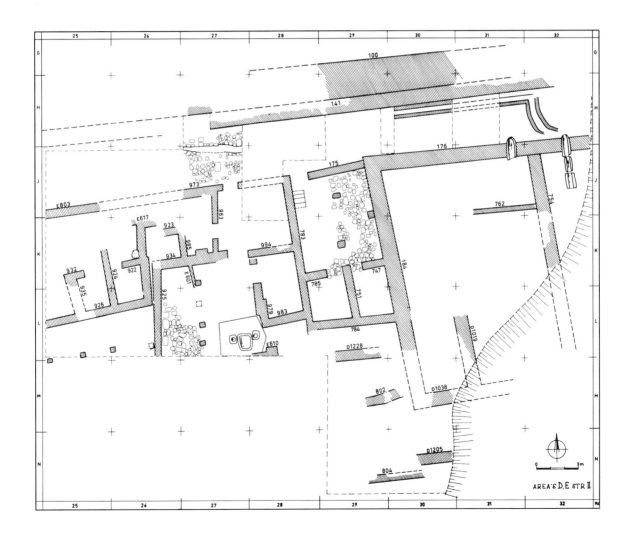

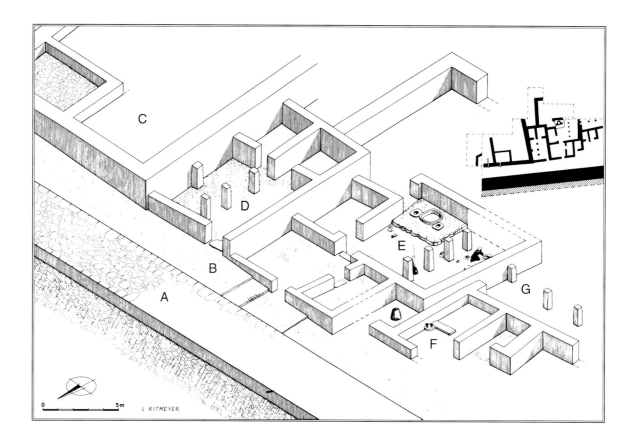

L RITMEYER

Fig. 8.6. Isometric drawing of architectural features in Areas D and E (Stratum II).

A: City wall
B: Street
C: Public building
D: Building 743
E: Building 950
F: Small piazza
G: Pillared building

Large quantities of pottery sherds, animal bones, and ash in the street accumulation provide evidence that refuse was dumped in the street. Among the sherds from the street were two stamped handles, one with a rosette stamp sealing and the other with a two-winged *lmlk* sealing. The rosette stamp is a royal Judean seal of the late seventh century, while the *lmlk* seal impression could either be a stray find from the previous stratum or a piece of evidence for the continued use of *lmlk* jars during the seventh century.

A Typical Private Dwelling (Building 743). A typical dwelling of the seventh century B.C.E. (Stratum II) was excavated adjoining the public structure of Area D on the west. The outer walls of this house (7.70 × 11.25 m) were preserved as a single line of large blocks on a foundation base of smaller stones. The entrance (1.25 m wide) into the dwelling from the street was located in the western corner of the northern wall facing the city wall. Directly inside the entrance, only three stone steps remained of a staircase that led to the roof or to additional rooms on the second floor.

The inner space of the building, divided by three monolithic pillars, provided access to two square rooms that served as sleeping quarters in the rear of the house. The pillars, typical of the period, were square (ca. 0.4 × 0.4 m) and up to 1.7 m high. The western half of the space directly inside the entrance had a beaten-earth floor, while the half to the east of the pillars was paved with flagstones. The flagstone side was roofed and provided shelter for the animals that were stabled there. The other half was either an open air courtyard or a roofed space for cooking and other household activities such as weaving.

The general plan of the house and its building technique are typical of Israelite houses, such as those at Tell Beit Mirsim, Tell en-Nasbeh, and Beth-Shemesh, although the location of the staircase and the two square room configuration in the rear of the house are rare.[5] This house seems to have been founded in the eighth century and probably belonged to a larger complex that included the *lmlk* building. The house was modified in Stratum II, when the western

Fig. 8.7. City wall, street, and Dwelling 743 in Area D.

wall of the public building (described above) became its eastern wall.

The house was destroyed in the massive conflagration that terminated Stratum II at the end of the seventh century B.C.E. The collapse of the building's brick superstructure buried a rich collection of pottery vessels and metal tools on its floor. This assemblage, after restoration, permitted a detailed study of the pottery repertoire of this dwelling. The ce-

Fig. 8.8. Pottery assemblage from Dwelling 743 (Stratum II).

Fig. 8.9. Storage jars, kraters, and cooking pots from Dwelling 743 (Stratum II).

ramic collection provided us with the first opportunity for the study of a regional variation of the pottery of this period, namely that of the Philistine city-states of the inner coastal plain and the lower Shephelah. About 90 pottery vessels were restored from sherds found in this house. These included 31 bowls, 6 kraters, 12 cooking pots, 12 storage jars, 7 jugs, 6 bottles, 7 juglets, 3 stands, 1 lamp, and 5 other vessels. Many pottery types are uncommon in Judah, but are similar to pottery forms in Iron Age II strata at Ekron and Ashdod. Among the finds was a pottery bottle with an

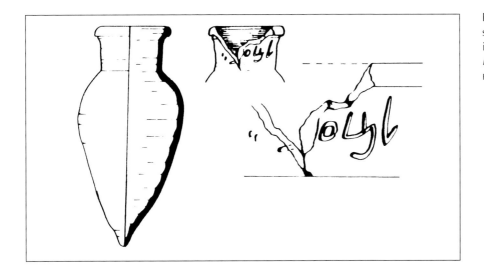

Fig. 8.10 (left). Assyrian-style bottle with inscription: "belonging to *ma*^c . . ." (seventh century B.C.E.).

Fig. 8.11 (below). Pottery assemblage and loom weights from Dwelling 743 (Stratum II).

incised inscription containing a private name of which only three letters were preserved: *lm^c*. . . , probably the beginning of a personal name, such as *le-ma^csyah* (belonging to *ma[^casiyahu]*). Near the entrance of the house several cooking pots and a stone weight inscribed with the word *pim* were found. A similar weight was found near the gate on the surface of the tell. Among other finds were an iron knife and a miniature bronze bell. Such a house probably accommodated a single family of six to eight persons.[6]

The Oil Press Building (Building 950). A complete house, adjoining the western wall of House 743 in Area D, was excavated in Area E. A large entrance hall (5 × 4.5 m) that may have served as a shop provided access from the street to this "Oil Press Building." An adjoining side room was equipped with an oven. A doorway opposite the street entrance led from the "shop" into the eastern half of a central space. The latter was divided by a row of four monolithic pillars into an eastern part with a beaten earth floor and a western part paved with cobblestones. A rectangular room bordered the space on the east. The unique feature of this building was an oil press that had been constructed in the southeastern quadrant of the central space. This is the first of two such oil presses we uncovered at Tel Batash. The oil press consisted of a large stone basin and two hollowed-out stone vats embedded in a plastered, stone-built platform. Two large stone weights with suspension holes were found in the location of their final use at the end of the eastern beam of the oil press structure. They were large conical stones with rounded rope holes for attaching them at their desired location on the beam; the larger, complete stone weighed 58 kg. Three stone rollers of graded sizes used for crushing the olives in the stone basin were also found in the room. To extract the olive oil, reed-woven baskets filled with the crushed olive "mash" from the basin were stacked over the round openings of the hollowed stone vats flanking the basin. A long wooden beam anchored in the rear wall of the room extended beyond the reed baskets; a series of attached stone weights provided adequate pressure to extract the oil from the mash. Small "sediment" cups in the base of the vats facilitated the removal of clean oil without disturbing any solid impurities that might have escaped with the oil from the mash in the baskets above.

Fig. 8.12. Oil press installation in the "Oil Press Building" in Area E, Stratum II (view to the north).

Following the pressing operation, the olive oil could be easily dipped from the vats with small dipper juglets into storage jars for transport, permanent storage, or possibly for direct sale in the front room adjoining the street.

In the western part of the building, beyond the row of pillars, two "torpedo" jars had been embedded with their flat stone lids flush with the stone floor. Channels in the floor apparently directed fluids from a large conglomerate "rubbing" stone near the adjoining wall to the jars. This special installation possibly was intended for the special care committed to the preparation of the ritual oil of the 'first-fruits' (*shemen katit* = ritually-pure oil, Exod 29:40).

The Oil Press Building, like the private dwelling on its east, was destroyed in an intense fire. Dozens of restorable pottery vessels characteristic of the late seventh century B.C.E. were recovered from this building.

Additional Structures in Area E. The remains of two more units were excavated to the west of the Oil Press

L RITMEYER 83

S 960

Fig. 8.14. Stone weight (used for pressing olive mash to extract oil) found near monolithic pillar in Building 950.

Fig. 8.13. Architect's reconstruction of oil press installation in Area E.

Building. The corner of a building with three monolithic pillars was exposed. The proportions of the building and the distance between the pillars suggested that this might have been a large storage depot of the type known from other Iron Age sites. Only full excavation of the building, however, could confirm this hypothesis.

North of this building, a single room opened onto a piazza bordering the street. At the eastern end of the piazza, two complete chalices were found on a small brick platform. A fragmentary cult vessel was recovered nearby. It is possible that this open area served as a small, local community cult center.

Residential/Industrial Complex in Area F. In Area F, 25 m west of Area E, two similar dwellings (each ca. 5.5 × 9 m) with a common wall were exposed. The plans of these

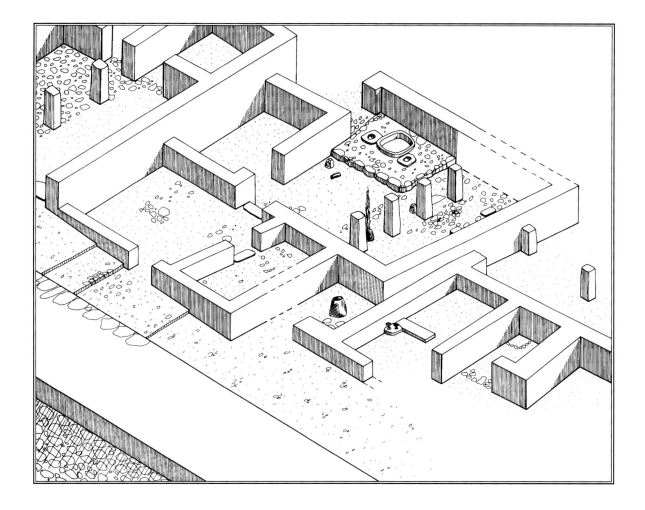

two buildings are comparable to Building 743 in Area D. An entrance led into a rectangular area divided lengthwise by a row of stone pillars. An additional room or two were situated at the rear of the building. In both buildings, the area west of the row of pillars was paved with cobblestones, while the space to the east and the rooms in the interior had beaten earth floors. A unique feature was a rounded pillar, 0.57 m in diameter, found in the western building. This is an exceptional feature, since all other pillars in Iron Age buildings in Israel are square. Both buildings had an oven in the eastern part of the courtyard. An unusual industrial installation against the northern wall of both buildings included a flat stone basin, with low sides and a drain spout opening toward the street. To the south of the trough was a stone vat. A third installation of this type was located just below surface soil beyond the western wall of the second house and

Fig. 8.15. Isometric drawing of architectural features adjoining "Oil Press Building" in Area E.

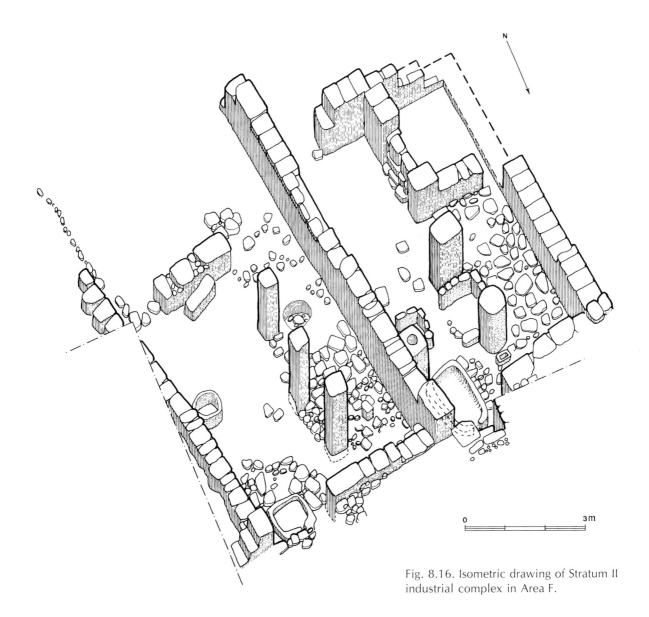

Fig. 8.16. Isometric drawing of Stratum II industrial complex in Area F.

may have belonged to a third house in this row. A similar installation was discovered at Ekron in the contemporary late seventh century B.C.E. house in Field III.[7] These installations must have been used in an industry, such as textile dyeing, in which disposal of undesirable liquids into the street or gutter was necessary.

Debris from both houses that were destroyed by fire yielded large quantities of broken pottery. The assemblage from the eastern building contained more than 67 restorable vessels, including 17 bowls, 3 "mortaria" bowls, 4 kraters,

4 cooking pots, 11–15 storage jars, 3 holemouth jars, 4 jugs, 15 juglets, 2 painted deep chalices, 1 four-handled deep "jar-amphora", 1 amphora, 1 imported Greek (Samian) amphora from the island of Samos, and 2 lamps. Three rosette seal impressions, of the type common in Judah towards the end of the Iron Age and probably all from the same jar, were also found in this house. (The jar could not be restored). The finds also included a unique iron spearhead with a shafted tang and a blade 42 cm long, as well as several other iron objects and iron lumps.

Architectural Complex and Oil Press in Area H

A large architectural complex of Stratum II was uncovered just below the surface and above the ruined public structures of Stratum III in Area H. The eastern limits of this complex and the city wall of this period were eroded away. The complex included two major units divided by a

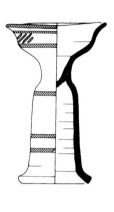

Fig. 8.18. Buildings and Stratum II industrial installations in Area F (view to north).

Fig. 8.17. Painted chalices from Area F.

0   10cm

Fig. 8.19. Pottery collection from Area F buildings in Stratum II.

main north-south wall of which a 16.7 m section was preserved. A doorway connecting the two units was located at its southern end. The eastern unit contained several large areas: a hall or an alley measuring 2.7 × 9.4 m, with a round, stone-built silo in its corner; two areas paved with stones (one measuring 3.5 × 7.5 m; the other, 2.7 × 5.0 m), and two additional rooms at the southern end of the area. The main space in this eastern wing contained a row of large stone pillar bases. Unfortunately, its eastern portion had been destroyed by erosion. This structure differed in plan from the private dwellings in Areas D, E, and F and may have served as a storehouse or mercantile center. The destruction layer in this area was thin, with most of its floor levels near topsoil.

The western wing of the complex also contained several units. In the south, the floor of a 3 m wide room or courtyard, well-paved with large stone slabs, was covered by a thick layer of burnt destruction debris with very few finds. To its north, another structure contained an excellent oil press installation, similar to but more elaborate than the Area E example. Its components were embedded in a 3.2 × 3.9 m raised stone platform, surrounded by walls on three sides. In its center was a monolithic crushing basin (0.8 × 1.3 m, 0.42 m deep) flanked by two stone pressing vats: one was round (outer diameter 0.98 m), the other, square (0.74 × 0.84 m). This square press is similar to those found in large numbers in the contemporary Level I at Tel Miqne-Ekron. The round type is similar to those found at other sites in the Shephelah, such as Tell Beit Mirsim. Both have a concave upper surface, probably shaped to hold a wooden frame for the baskets of crushed olive mash. The stone pressing vats collected the extracted olive oil during the pressing operation. Two niches for anchoring the installation's long wooden beam were preserved in the southern wall behind the presses. Three stone weights were found in position near the presumed end of the eastern beam. The biblical reference to "the House of the Beam" (*beth ha-bad*) has been clarified by the use of the wooden beam in such installations of the domestic olive oil industry.

Our press is typical of the Iron Age oil presses in the Shephelah, now known in large numbers at Tel Miqne.[8] The Tel Miqne installations, however, lack the stone platforms that are characteristic of both oil presses excavated at Timnah. It appears that at Ekron the approach to the raised presses and the vats was more suitable for work done while standing, while at Timnah the workers tended to the pressing operation and the dipping of the oil while crouching. The 2-m space between the back wall and the center of the stone presses also

Fig. 8.20. General view of Area H with oil press building of Stratum II in foreground (view to east).

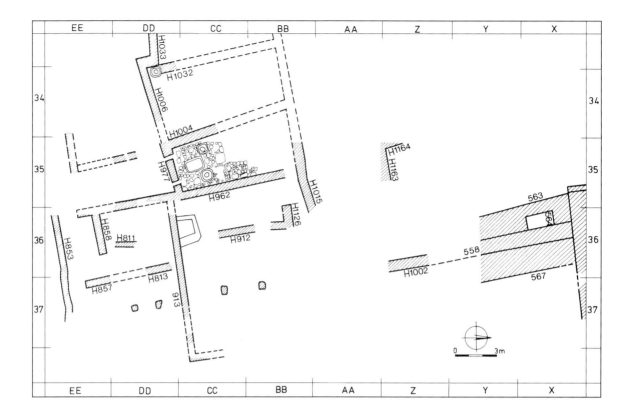

Fig. 8.21. Schematic plan of structures in Area H in relation to gate (lower right) in Area C (Stratum II).

lacks any parallel at Tel Miqne, where the presses are located closer to the back wall. This feature at Timnah, while reducing the leverage potential of the beams, may have allowed for greater pressure control. Generally, however, these two features of our oil presses seem to suggest a less efficient operation than that of the presses at Ekron, in spite of the great resemblance between the two. Another unique feature of our oil press is a large flat stone located at the front edge of the platform, opposite the crushing vat. A large broken monolithic pillar found fallen near this flat stone must have stood on it. This pillar probably supported the roof of the structure, but could also have served as a divider between the two beams. No roller stones of the Area E type identified as crushers were found in Area H.

Many pottery vessels were found in a destruction layer in an open area west of the oil press. In this area, a round stone vat similar to the example in the oil press had been incorporated in a corner formed by two late Stratum II walls in secondary use. The location of this vat suggests that oil presses of this type were already in use during an earlier phase of Stratum II. Similar developments at Ekron suggest

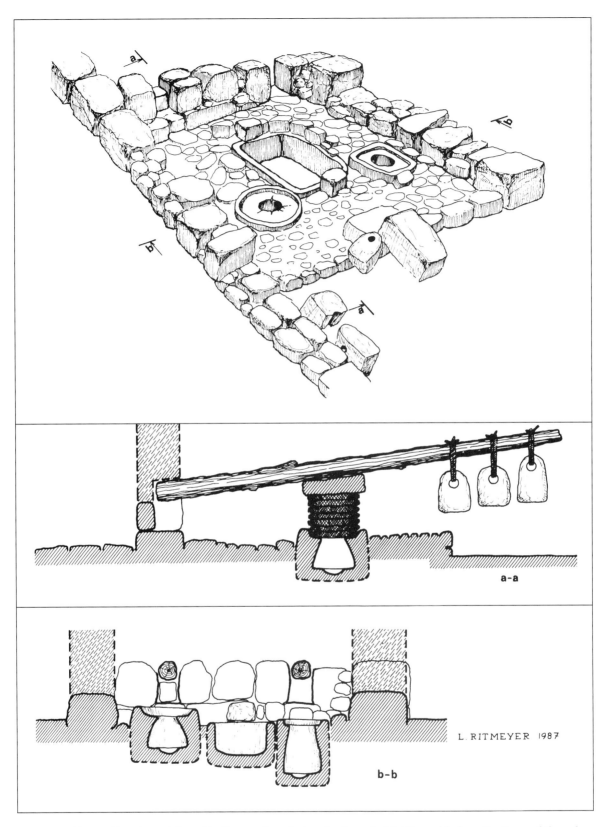

Fig. 8.22. Above: Drawing of Area H oil press installation (as found). Middle and below: Sections of the oil press installation with reconstruction of the use of weights and beam in extracting oil from woven baskets filled with crushed olive mash (note line of sections: a–a; b–b).

that some olive presses used during the mid-seventh century were abandoned in the later years of that century.

The Urban Plan

The extensive Iron Age residential and industrial areas excavated at Timnah along the northern and eastern crests of the mound provide a superb example of urban planning in Iron Age II Palestine. In some ways, it resembles the city planning of Judean cities such as Tell en-Nasbeh, Tell Beit Mirsim, Beth-Shemesh, and Beersheba.[9] Timnah's town plan, however, differs in a number of important details. The straight line of the city wall, the street along the northern wall and the straight facade of buildings along the street were dictated by the square shape of the preexisting mound. The wide street that separates the city wall from Timnah's residential quarter is unique and does not appear in other Judean cities, where the inner rooms of pillared houses were often integrated in a casemate wall surrounding the city. It appears that there were different quarters in the city. The gate complex and the large piazza inside it were probably used as a center for public affairs and commerce. The complex in Area H, south of the gate, was probably an industrial and commercial area. At the highest point of the mound, the northeastern corner, a large public building possibly served as a barrack. To its west, the street running along the city wall was lined by private dwellings with home industries, including the production of olive oil and textile manufacturing. The houses were of similar size and nature, hinting at the more or less egalitarian social status of the inhabitants in this quarter. A small piazza in this area may have been used for local cult ceremonies.

The house plans are similar to those of many Iron Age dwellings excavated earlier. The main space divided by a row of monolithic pillars was apparently a standard architectural feature, although individual room arrangements adjoining the court were dictated by particular needs. A major question concerning these houses is whether the ground floor was completely roofed, or whether one part of it remained an unroofed courtyard. It has traditionally been thought that the central area with the pillars was an unroofed courtyard, left open to facilitate the use of ovens.

Fig. 8.23. Stratum II jug from Area H.

Indeed, the frequent discovery of ovens in these spaces indicates that they were unroofed. On the other hand, the beaten earth floors in these areas show no signs of the deterioration that could be expected to occur during the rainy winter season, and this may indicate that the entire ground floor of these houses was roofed.[10]

Timnah Within Its Economic and Cultural Setting

Olive Oil Production. The elaborate oil press in Area H and the simpler one in Area E demonstrate the economic importance of olive oil production in the city during the seventh century B.C.E. Comparable oil presses in the Shephelah are known at Gezer, Beth-Shemesh, and Tell Beit Mirsim (where W. F. Albright erroneously identified them as "dyeing vats").[11] Rock-cut oil presses featuring similar technology have also been found in many highland sites.

Evidence of the most elaborate Iron Age oil industry known, however, has been discovered at Ekron, just 6 km southwest of Timnah (Ekron Stratum I is contemporary with Timnah Stratum II). Surface survey and excavations at Ekron identified 113 oil-press complexes similar to that in Area H at Timnah. Studies of Ekron's oil industry have estimated an annual production level of a thousand tons. Such production would have required more than 50,000 dunams (12,500 acres) of olive groves within a radius of 10–20 km surrounding the town, a minimal employment of 2,000 workers, and 4,000 sq m of storage space to accommodate approximately 48,000 storage jars.[12] These are minimal estimates, since many more oil presses at Ekron are probably still unexcavated. During this period Ekron grew dramatically, from an area of ten acres during the tenth-eighth centuries B.C.E. (approximately the size of Timnah) to forty acres and an additional ten acres beyond the tell proper. This growth was presumably related to the development of the region's oil industry. S. Gitin, co-director of the Tel Miqne excavations, assumes that the industrial zone occupied at least twenty percent of the city's total area.

The prosperity related to this urban expansion at Ekron and a comparably vibrant commercial center at Timnah must be attributed to external commercial exploitation. The restoration of Ekron following the Assyrian invasion in 701 B.C.E.

Fig. 8.24. Assyrian painted bottle.

and Assyrian economic stimulation resulted in a revitalized town that soon expanded beyond any previous limits. The period of the *Pax Assyriaca*, lasting during most of the seventh century B.C.E. (until ca. 630 when Assyrian power declined), resulted in a vibrant economy and wider international trade relations. Ekron probably took advantage of the situation to develop a thriving industry and long-range trade in olive oil within the framework of the Assyrian empire. It became a large independent city-state with tremendous economic strength.[13] The most obvious market for its oil was Egypt, though the presence of Eastern Greek, Phoenician, and Transjordanian pottery at Ekron, Timnah, and Meṣad Hashavyahu on the coast west of Ekron suggests that oil was exported to other Mediterranean markets as well. The integration of Ekron's economy with those of other Assyrian vassal city-states stimulated not only urban development but agrarian industries. During much of the seventh century B.C.E., Timnah presumably benefited from the prosperity of its larger neighbor Ekron, though it played a lesser role in the oil industry and trade. Timnah would have enjoyed the commercial benefits of its strategic location on the major lateral trade and communications route across Judah to the Transjordan (Ammon, Moab and Edom).

The dissolution of Assyrian control in Philistia and the Shephelah after 730 B.C.E. resulted in a gradual decline in the oil industry and trade, as is demonstrated by the secondary use of stone basins and presses for non-oil related functions, such as watering troughs and wall construction. This phenomenon is common to both Ekron and Timnah.

Thus, commercial and political developments in the immediate vicinity clearly had a bearing on Timnah's urban and industrial development. The olive oil industry must have been a very important factor in the economy of the entire region during the seventh century.

Textile Industry. Thirty to fifty clay loom weights were recovered from each of the domestic buildings excavated in Stratum II Timnah. These weights were used in vertical looms, like those portrayed in Greek vase paintings. The recovery of these weights from all the houses can leave no doubt that weaving was a most important home industry in Timnah, as in many other Iron Age cities where such weights have been found.

Fig. 8.25. Functional loom constructed with Timnah weights.

Fig. 8.26. Loom weights scattered on floor of Dwelling 743 (Stratum II).

The installations found in Area F houses, consisting of stone vats and flat stone basins with drainage spouts oriented to the street, appear to have been used in the cleaning, dyeing, and final treatment of wool in preparation for spinning and weaving. Though this evidence for spinning and weaving may only reflect "domestic" industries, this thriving textile production at Timnah may be related to the necessity to pay tribute to the Assyrian rulers of the region. Assyrian lists of tribute from Philistine cities include linen suits, robes, and tent cloth and reflect Assyrian interests in local textiles. The payment of tribute may well have required the manufacture of finished woolen garments and other textiles to meet specific taxation quotas imposed by the Assyrian overlords on each town.[14]

If the olive oil industry at Timnah, as in modern times, required only seasonal involvement, ample opportunity existed for scheduling and integrating the available work force into other local industries. The olive oil and textile industries thus appear to have been technically and chronologically compatible, perhaps conducted in the same installations.[15] The seasonal shearing of sheep during the olive "off-season" provided a complementary industry in commercial centers such as Timnah and Ekron.

The Ceramic Evidence. The violent destruction of the Stratum II buildings buried large accumulations of finds in each of the houses excavated. The repertoire includes hundreds of pottery vessels, seal impressions, metal objects and stone weights. These have become an important source for the study of the relationship of Judah and Philistia during the late Iron Age.

The pottery may be divided into five main groups:
a. types characteristic of Philistia
b. types characteristic of the kingdom of Judah
c. types common to both Judah and Philistia
d. types that resemble Assyrian shapes
e. imported pottery including Phoenician, Transjordanian, and Greek vessels.

The uniqueness of the scope and nature of the pottery assemblage may reflect Timnah's location in a border zone between neighboring geopolitical units, each exerting important influence on the inhabitants of a buffer zone. Some of the vessels have unique or very rare shapes.

The late Philistine assemblage finds its closest parallels at Ekron (Stratum I), at Meṣad Hashavyahu (dated to the end of the seventh century B.C.E.), and to some extent at Ashdod, where a somewhat different regional variety can be defined. Timnah's pottery probably reflects the potters' tradition of the kingdom of Ekron, which differed in many details from Ashdod preferences during the Iron Age II. However, in contrast to Ekron, the assemblage from Timnah contains more Judean forms. Most Stratum II houses contained examples of *lmlk* jars (Type 484, according to Tufnell's typology at Lachish), as well as jars considered to be later developments of the *lmlk* jars though differing in details of shape and clay color (Type 483, usually light gray, sometimes with rosette seal impressions).[16] Timnah Stratum II yielded six rosette seal impressions on handles of similar jars, two of them probably from a single jar. However, none of the restored *lmlk* jars from Stratum II were sealed with the royal stamp, though two fragmentary handles sealed

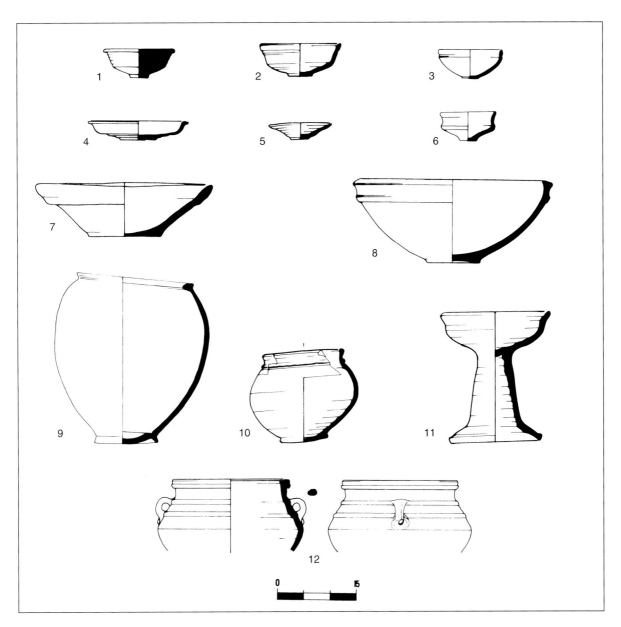

Fig. 8.27. Selection of pottery from Stratum II: bowls and kraters.

No.	Registration No.	Locus	Type of Vessel	Description
1	7573/2	743	Bowl	Brown clay; gray core; gray grits; red slip inside
2	7185	743	Bowl	Reddish clay; few white small grits
3	7579/2	746	Bowl	Reddish clay; few white small grits
4	1146	142	Bowl	Gray clay; gray core; black slip; well burnished inside and outside
5	7534	743	Bowl	Gray clay; few white grits
6	7559	779	Bowl	Brown clay; gray core; few white small grits
7	F6229	F621	Krater	Sandy yellowish clay; few white small grits
8	7136	745	Krater	Sandy brown clay; gray core; white small grits
9	7193	743	Krater	Reddish clay; gray core; few white grits
10	7553/3	779	Krater	Yellowish clay; gray core; white and black small grits
11	9056	910	Chalice	Reddish clay; gray core; white wash
12	7579/1	746	Krater	Reddish-orange clay; yellowish core; red slip inside and outside

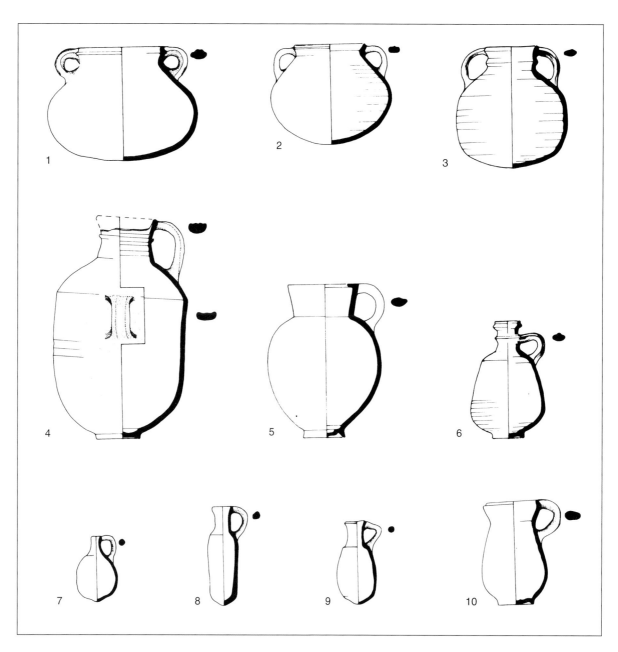

Fig. 8.28. Selection of pottery from Stratum II: cooking pots, jugs, and juglets.

No.	Registration No.	Locus	Type of Vessel	Description
1	7577	778	Cooking pot	Brown-reddish clay; gray core; many white and brown grits
2	7565	778	Cooking pot	Brown-reddish clay; gray core; white small and large grits
3	7542	779	Cooking pot	Brown reddish clay; gray core; white small and large grits
4	7562	779	Jug	Yellowish clay; few white and brown grits
5	7555/2	781	Jug	Reddish clay; gray core; white small grits
6	7554/3	743	Jug	Gray clay; gray core; white small grits
7	7137	746	Juglet	Brown-orange clay; white small and large grits
8	7220	743	Juglet	Brown clay; gray core; white small and large grits
9	7190	743	Juglet	Brown-orange clay; brown small grits
10	7114	743	Juglet	Brown-gray clay; white small and large grits

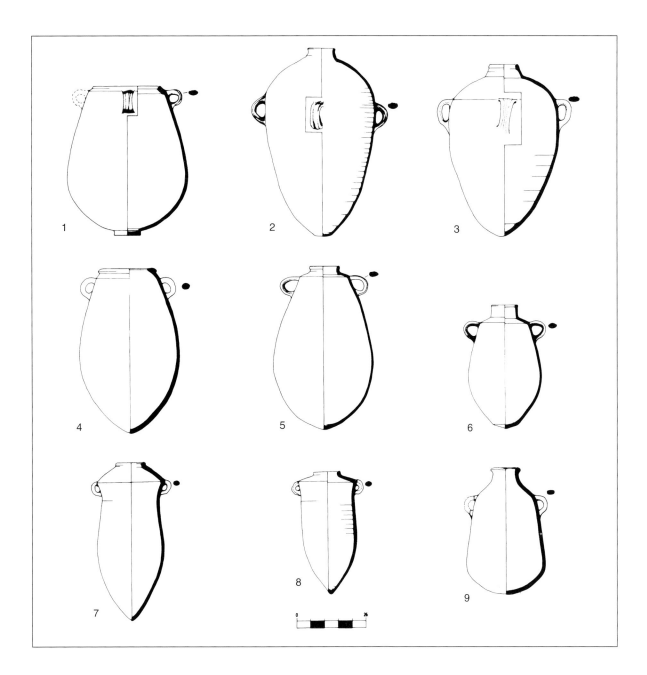

Fig. 8.29. Selection of pottery from Stratum II: storage jars.

No.	Registration No.	Locus	Description
1	7589	776	Reddish-brown clay; gray core; white small grits
2	1231	173	Brown-yellowish clay; gray core; white small grits
3	7269	734	Reddish-brown clay; brown core; many white small grits
4	1235	173	Brown clay; white small grits
5	7598	743	Pinkish clay; gray core; white and brown small grits
6	7189	753	Pinkish clay; brown core; many white small grits
7	9560	960	Brown-sandy clay
8	9404	960	Brown-sandy clay
9	9456	946	Brown-reddish clay; gray core

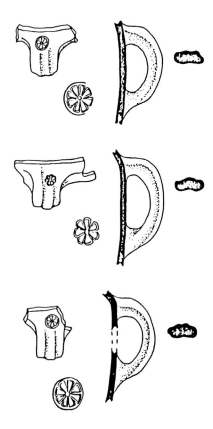

Fig. 8.30. Rosette stamp seal impressions on storage jar handles.

with two-winged *lmlk* seal impressions were found. The surprising find of complete *lmlk* jars in the late seventh century B.C.E. context of Stratum II can be explained in several ways:

1. Such jars may have continued in use throughout the seventh century B.C.E. This seems doubtful in view of the homogeneity of the clay and production technique. Chemical analysis has shown that all the *lmlk* jars were produced at a single production center. Thus, all the *lmlk* jars were presumably produced during a relatively short period preceding Sennacherib's invasion in 701.

2. The jars found in Stratum II were produced together with the other *lmlk* jars during the late eighth century and somehow continued in use throughout the seventh century B.C.E. This possibility seems legitimate since the jars were probably used for storing products in royal storehouses, where careful handling could have assured their continuous use over a long period. It is possible that even at Timnah such a royal storehouse, escaping destruction during Sennacherib's invasion, could have remained in use during the following century.

3. Such jars arrived at Timnah during the seventh century from other locations, where they had been preserved after Hezekiah's reign. The prime candidate for such a place is Jerusalem itself, which survived the 701 B.C.E. Assyrian invasion and where thousands of such jars were probably housed in royal storage centers. During the seventh century such jars certainly continued in use and were distributed to various other sites.[17]

One of the major unsolved problems is whether after 630 B.C.E. Timnah became a Judean town, during the rule of Josiah, or whether it remained a Philistine town as part of the kingdom of Ekron. The pottery assemblage shows a unique combination of Judean and late Philistine pottery forms and other objects. The similarity of contemporary cultural remains at Timnah and at Meṣad Hashavyahu, a fortress on the coast west of Tel Batash suggests a common culture.[18] The Hebrew letters found at Meṣad Hashavyahu may indicate that, during the time of Josiah, Judah controlled a portion of the coastal plain, with the Sorek Valley serving as one of the most important routes to the coast.[19] This may account for the vitality of Timnah's economy during this pe-

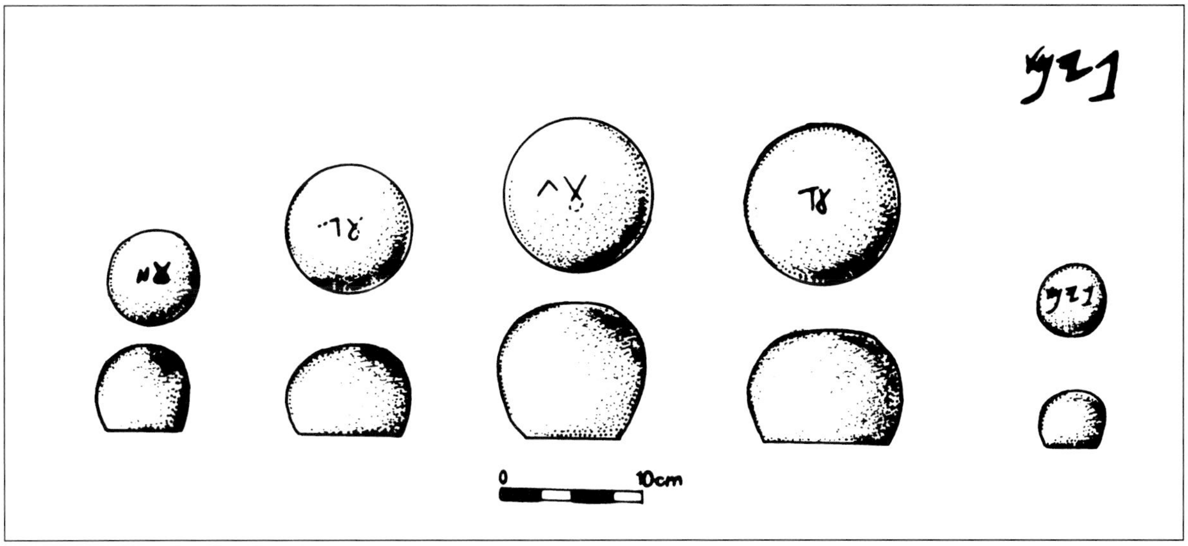

Fig. 8.31. Series of commercial weights of Judean type (*pym* and *shekel* units) (Stratum II).

riod. However, the combination of coastal forms and Judean forms of pottery vessels indicates the possibility that even though Timnah may have been under Judean control, a large part of its population remained local "Philistines," who were naturally related to the inhabitants of the great city-state of Ekron nearby.

Seal Impressions and Weights. Timnah's relations with the Judean kingdom are also reflected in a group of seal impressions and stone weights. The seal impressions include two examples of two-winged *lmlk* stamped handles (one reading *lmlk skh*, the other illegible) found in a clear Stratum II context. The six rosette seal impressions found on Stratum II jar handles have eight petals. They are characteristic of late seventh century Judah and may have replaced the *lmlk* seals as royal seals during this period.[20]

The stone weights are all dome-shaped with flat bases, characteristic of Judean types. Three of them are inscribed with the word *pym*. Their weights vary slightly: 7.88, 7.72, and 8.02 grams. A two-shekel weight is marked with a II ɣ sign. Its weight is 22.78 grams. A four-shekel weight (No. 6160) marked ᒣ ɣ weighs 43 grams. Two eight-shekel weights were found (Nos. 9422, 9732). One (91.2 grams) is marked with the usual sign ᐱ ɣ, and the other (91.16) has an unusual sign T ɣ. It should be noted that these weights are fairly consistent with the averages generally attributed to such specimens.[21] The weights, scattered throughout the

Stratum II area, indicate Timnah's strong economic relationship with the kingdom of Judah.

Timnah's Demise as an Urban Center

The fate of Timnah following the end of Assyrian control in ca. 630 B.C.E. is not clear. As we have already noted, the town may have come under Judean jurisdiction during Josiah's attempt to challenge Egyptian encroachment beyond the coastal plain into the Shephelah and the central hill country. Ekron appears to have fallen under Egyptian domination for a brief period before its destruction by Nebuchadnezzar in 603 B.C.E. Though two construction phases were observed in a few places in the Stratum II buildings, they may suggest nothing more than a degree of inner development and change in the city during the seventh century B.C.E. However, there is no indication of general destruction and structural change between 701 and ca. 600 B.C.E., when the Stratum II city was destroyed by fire.

Fig. 8.32. Extent of the Babylonian Empire (sixth century B.C.E.).

Whatever their final political relationship, Timnah and Ekron met a similar fate. Between 609 and 587 B.C.E., several military campaigns penetrated the Shephelah, each

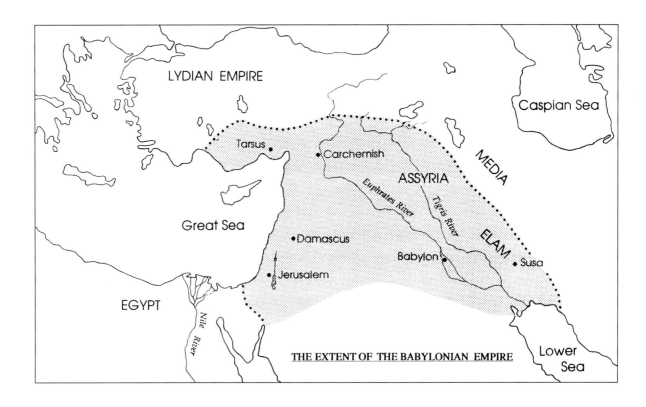

Fig. 8.33. Industrial installation (probable wine press) in Area D.

with the potential for destroying Timnah.[22] In 609 the Egyptian army under Pharaoh Necho passed nearby on its northward route to an ill-fated Assyrian campaign, and until 605 the Egyptians maintained a semblance of control over the coastal plain. In 605 B.C.E. Nebuchadnezzar conquered Ashkelon. He invaded Philistia again in 603 and 601. Additional Babylonian invasions targeted Judah, which finally surrendered in 586 B.C.E. An Aramaic letter from Saqqara, perhaps originating in Ekron or another city in Philistia, indicates the severe tension in the region during the Babylonian invasions.[23] Timnah and Ekron were probably destroyed during the campaigns of 605–601 B.C.E. Both were conquered and destroyed in a massive conflagration by the Babylonian armies.

Slight traces of a squatters' settlement existed on the destruction debris of Timnah. An industrial installation, probably a wine press, was constructed on the remains of House 743. It consisted of a circular stone structure, with a plastered central surface (ca. 1.5 m in diameter) that allowed drainage of the grape juices from this "treading" surface into the end of a rectangular stone vat (0.7 × 1.3 m). A hole at the base of the vat's other end allowed drainage into storage jars for the transfer of the collected juices. Restorable

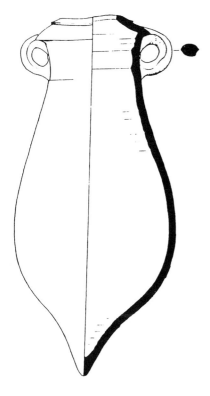

Fig. 8.34. A storage jar from the end of the Iron Age or the Persian period.

remains of two storage jars and a cooking pot recovered beside the stone vat were dated to the end of the Iron Age. These vessels are Judean in type and may indicate a minor Judean occupation at the site after its extensive destruction by the Babylonians, although this suggestion may require further clarification.

The Persian Period

The few scattered remains of the Persian period discovered on the surface of the mound suggested the presence of a modest occupation on the tell during the fifth–fourth centuries B.C.E. The gate area also provided evidence of the re-use of the gate passage during this period. A drainage trench cut through the gate area probably drained an area in the center of the site, where more substantial buildings might have existed. Several refuse pits were cut during the Persian period into earlier Iron Age occupation layers. One of the pits contained the bones of a small dog. These bones, identified by Dr. B. Hesse, had been thrown into the pit rather than intentionally buried as in the Persian period dog cemetery discovered at Ashkelon.[24]

Endnotes

1. B. Oded, "Neighbors on the West," in *The World History of the Jewish People, Vol. 4* (ed. A. Malamat; First Series: Ancient Times; Jerusalem: Massada, 1979) 222–46; I. Eph'al, "Assyrian Dominion in Palestine," in *ibid.*, 276–89; J. Bright, *A History of Israel* (Philadelphia: Westminster, 1981) 195–228; J. M. Miller and J. H. Hayes, *A History of Ancient Israel and Judah* (Philadelphia: Westminster, 1986) 149–217.

2. E. D. Oren, "Ziklag—A Biblical City on the Edge of the Negev," *BA* 45 (1982) 159–60; idem, "Ethnicity and Regional Archaeology: The Western Negev under Assyrian Rule," in *Biblical Archaeology Today* (ed. A. Biran and J. Aviram; Jerusalem: Israel Exploration Society, 1993) 102–5; R. Reich, "The Identification of the 'Sealed *Karu* of Egypt'," *IEJ* 34 (1984) 32–38.

3. B. Brandel and R. Reich, "Gezer under Assyrian Rule," *PEQ* 117 (1985) 41–54; S. Gitin and T. Dothan, "The Rise and Fall of Ekron of the Philistines," *BA* 50 (1987) 197–222; S. Gitin, "Tel Miqne-Ekron: A Type-Site for the Inner Coastal Plain in the Iron Age II Period," in *Recent Excavations in Israel: Studies in Iron Age Archaeology* (AASOR 49; ed. S. Gitin and W. G. Dever; Winona Lake: Eisenbrauns, 1989) 23–58.

4. R. S. Lamon and G. M. Shipton, *Megiddo I: Seasons of 1925–34, Strata I-V* (Oriental Institute Publications 42; Chicago: University of Chicago, 1939) 74–83; Y. Yadin, *Hazor, the Head of All Those Kingdoms* (Schweich Lectures of the British Academy, 1970; London: Oxford Univer-

sity Press, 1972) 160; Z. Herzog, "Settlement and Fortification Planning in the Iron Age," in *The Architecture of Ancient Israel from the Prehistoric to the Persian Periods* (ed. A. Kempinski and R. Reich; Jerusalem: Israel Exploration Society, 1992) 265–74.

5. Y. Shiloh, "The Four-Room House—Its Situation and Function in the Israelite City," *IEJ* 20 (1970) 180–90; W. F. Albright, *The Excavation of Tell Beit Mirsim, III: The Iron Age* (AASOR 21–22; New Haven, 1943) 50, House NW21A-9; Ehud Netzer, "Domestic Architecture in the Iron Age," in *The Architecture of Ancient Israel*, 193–201.

6. Shiloh estimated eight persons for a similar dwelling. See Y. Shiloh, "The Population of Iron Age Palestine in the Light of a Sample Analysis of Urban Plans, Areas, and Population Density," *BASOR* 239 (1980) 25–35.

7. Dothan and Gitin, "The Rise and Fall of Ekron," 207–9.

8. Gitin, "Tel Miqne-Ekron," 32; D. Eitam and A. Shomroni, "Research of the Oil Industry During the Iron Age at Tel Miqne—A Preliminary Report," in *Olive Oil in Antiquity* (Conference Reports 1987; ed. D. Eitam; Haifa: University of Haifa, Israel Oil Industry Museum, Dagon Museum, 1987) 37–56.

9. Y. Shiloh, "Elements in the Development of Town Planning in the Israelite City," *IEJ* 28 (1978) 36–51.

10. This is the view of Netzer ("Domestic Architecture"); see also L. E. Stager, "The Archaeology of the Family in Ancient Israel," *BASOR* 260 (1985) 1–35.

11. E. Grant and G. E. Wright, *Ain Shems Excavations, Vol. 5* (Haverford: 1938) pls. 19:3, 21:1, 73: 6, fig. 9.

12. D. Eitam, "Olive Oil Production during the Biblical Period," in *Olive Oil in Antiquity*, 16–36; S. Gitin, "Tel Miqne-Ekron"; idem, "Tel Miqne-Ekron in the 7th Century B.C.: City Plan Development and the Oil Industry," in *Olive Oil in Antiquity*, 81–105.

13. S. Gitin, "Tel Miqne-Ekron," 23–58.

14. D. C. Browning, *The Textile Industry of Iron Age Timnah and Its Regional and Socioeconomic Contexts: A Literary and Artifactual Analysis* (Unpublished dissertation; Fort Worth, Tx: Southwestern Baptist Theological Seminary, 1988) 73–79, 156–62.

15. D. Eitam, "The Oil Industry During the Iron Age at Tel Miqne."

16. O. Tufnell, *Lachish III (Tell ed-Duweir): The Iron Age* (London: Oxford University Press, 1953) 316, pl. 95.

17. A. Mazar, D. Amit, and Z. Ilan, "The 'Border Road' between Michmash and Jericho and the Excavations at Horvat Shilhah," *Eretz-Israel* 17 (1984) 147–48 (Hebrew).

18. J. Naveh, "The Excavations at Meṣad Hashavyahu," *IEJ* 12 (1962) 89–113.

19. For a different view see N. Na'aman, "The Kingdom of Judah under Josiah," *Tel Aviv* 18 (1991) 3–71.

20. J. Cahill, "Rosette Stamp Seal Impressions from Judah," *IEJ* (forthcoming).

21. O. Tufnell, *Lachish III*, 350; W. G. Dever, "Iron Age Epigraphic Material from the Area of Khirbet el-Kom," *HUCA* 40–41 (1970) 174–86; R. B. Y. Scott, "Weights and Measures of the Bible," *BA* 22 (1959) 37, 38; R. Kletter, "The Inscribed Weights of the Kingdom of Judah," *Tel Aviv* 18 (1991) 121–63.

22. A. Malamat, "The Last Kings of Judah and the Fall of Jerusalem," *IEJ* 18 (1968) 137–156; idem, "Josiah's Bid for Armageddon," *Journal of the Ancient Near East Society of Columbia University* 5 (Gaster Festschrift; 1973: 267–78; idem, "The Twilight of Judah in the Egyptian-Babylonian Maelstrom," *VT Supplement* 28 (1975) 123–45.

23. B. Porten, "The Identity of King Adon," *BA* 44 (1981) 36–52.

24. P. Wapnish and B. Hesse, "The Ashkelon Dog Burials," *BA* 56 (1993) 55–80.

Appendix 1 The Expedition Program

The Daily Schedule

Two decades of observing and participating in archaeological field work had convinced us that volunteer participation in excavation programs could be enhanced and made significantly more meaningful by providing more pleasant living conditions and a strong educational emphasis. The need for an effective field school that would teach, train, and give our American students opportunities for pursuing archaeological studies on a graduate level was a primary concern. It was essential that the field work be a pleasant learning experience that would broaden interest and appreciation for the history and culture of the region, both ancient and present.

The expedition's daily work schedule was planned to provide working conditions conducive to positive training in the field and adequate leisure and learning time in camp to ensure an enjoyable and profitable overall archaeological experience. The following schedule was observed:

4:00 am	Wake Up Time
4:15	Early Morning Breakfast at the Shoresh Hotel
4:30	Departure for the Excavation Site
5:00	Commencement of Daily Work Assignments at the Site
8:30	Breakfast in the Field (30 minutes)
11:30	End of Field Work—Departure for Camp
1:00 pm	Lunch in Camp at Shoresh Hotel
2:00	Siesta Time
4:30	Afternoon Tea Time
5:00	Academic Program, Lectures, Training Sessions for Volunteers; Pottery Analysis for Staff Members
6:30	Supper in Shoresh Hotel Dining Room
7:30	Relaxation, Office Work, Field Reports, Analysis

The educational opportunities of an extended stay in the Holy Land required an integration of field work on the excavation site, procedures and techniques of evaluation and record keeping in the camp, and a lecture-format academic program of relevant historical and cultural subjects. Since the Timnah Expedition intentionally was designed as a field school, the academic program offered credit courses for both graduate and undergraduate students. Prerequisite reading required of all participants was intended to ensure a common foundation of perception of archaeological objectives. Staff members with developed specialization annually complemented a long list of internationally recognized archaeological specialists and scholars who contributed to the success of the academic program during the Expedition's twelve seasons. Lecture topics highlighted the historical geography of the Holy Land, archaeological sites and periods, the history and excavations of Tel Batash (Timnah), and modern Israel within its Near Eastern setting. Guided tours in The Israel Museum and Rockefeller Museum, archaeologically-oriented walking tours in Jerusalem including the Temple Mount, the Cardo, and the Jewish Quarter were integral aspects of the on-site training provided for participants each year.

The Volunteers

Fig. A.1. Excavation team (1985) on the remains of Timnah's gate (Area C).

The dedication of its volunteer force was one of the Timnah project's most obvious strengths. Not only did the volunteers pay their full travel and board-and-room expenses, but the nature of their integration into

Fig. A.2. 1989 Timnah volunteers depart for Israel Museum tour.

Fig. A.3. Visitors at Timnah excavation: (left to right) Trude Dothan (seated), Benjamin Mazar, Amihai Mazar, Nahum Avigad, Sy Gitin, Avi Eitan, Joseph Aviram.

Fig. A.4. Professor Yigael Yadin
discussing results of the excavation with
directors Amihai Mazar and George
Kelm.

Fig. A.5. Breakfast on the tell.

Fig. A.6. Keeping the
excavation "on the level."

and personal commitment to the expedition's specific scientific objectives and purposes of the daily assignments were exemplary. Their interest in and compliance with the broader archaeological and technical aims of their supervisors and directors and the quality of their work received regular praise from visiting archaeologists and other project administrators experienced in volunteer operations. During our twelve seasons, more than 600 volunteers and staff members from thirty-three states of the Union and at least twelve foreign countries and territories participated, many of them returning year after year. At least sixty volunteers participated in two to eight seasons of work, a continuity that contributed significantly to the integration and supervision of the digging process in the individual work areas.

The diversity of the volunteer group contributed greatly to the vitality of social and intellectual interchange during work and leisure times. Cultural interaction, beyond the integration of Israeli volunteers and our camp setting at the Shoresh Hotel in the Judean Hills, was provided by volunteers from Canada, Australia, England, Switzerland, West Germany, Republic of South Africa, Korea, Japan, Puerto Rico, Haiti, and the Panama Canal Zone. Though initial recruitment was directed primarily toward potential student volunteers, both graduate and undergraduate, the growing participation of "lay" volunteers, with their diversity of backgrounds and professional experience, ultimately was viewed not only as a meaningful but also very desirable force in achieving both archaeological and sociocultural objectives. Many of these volunteers, though "retired," proved their commitment and value in becoming our best and most reliable workers. Among them were medical doctors, university, college, and seminary professors, nurses, company presidents, geologists, public and high school teachers, chaplains, writers, engineering consultants, ministers, engineers, a nuclear physicist, computer analysts, an orthopedic atelier, a medical student, a geophysicist, secretaries, bookkeepers, and homemakers.

Fig. A.7. 1986 excavation work force on the tell.

Fig. A.8. 1979 excavation group at Shoresh Hotel, the expedition "First Class" camp.

The success of the volunteer program, in large measure, must be attributed to the personnel and services of the Shoresh Hotel, which became our expedition camp and for twelve years provided excellent facilities and services for our work both in their kind and generous provision for our physical needs and desires during each season and for storage of the expedition's equipment and supplies during the rest of the year.

Educational Travel

The Timnah theme which characterized the expedition's academic program was "Education through International Adventure." In addition to comprehensive sightseeing in Israel each year, the travel program included stopovers on either the incoming or outgoing portion of travel to Israel that enhanced the participants' interest and knowledge of other countries with sites and museums of archaeological significance.

The twelve seasons of field experience were complemented by the following travel schedule:

1977: Italy – Greece – Israel
1978: Israel – Greece – London – Aegean Cruise
1979: Israel – Greece – London
1981: Jordan – Israel – Cairo – Amsterdam
1982: Vienna – Cairo – Israel
1983: London – Vienna – Israel – Jordan – Amsterdam
1984: Greece – Israel
1985: Italy – Israel
1986: Greece – Israel – Amsterdam
1987: Israel – Sinai – Cairo – Switzerland
1988: Greece – Israel – Greek Island Cruise
1989: Israel

Fig. A.9. Potter/Restorer Orah Mazar and Registrar/Research Assistant Nava Panitz-Cohen in the Institute of Archaeology at the Hebrew University.

Fig. A.10. Linda L. Kelm, pottery restorer and museum curator, restoring pottery in the laboratory of the Charles D. Tandy Center for Archaeological Research.

Fig. A.11. Fort Worth City Manager Doug Harman visits the Tandy Archaeological Museum.

Fig. A.12. Timnah displays in Charles D. Tandy Archaeological Museum in the SWBTS library.

Archaeological Museum

The most meaningful continuing benefit of the Timnah project for Southwestern Seminary, as the primary sponsoring institution, was the establishment of the Charles D. Tandy Archaeological Museum in the seminary library. This museum displays representative artifacts from the excavation that illustrate the scope of the excavation and clarify the history and culture of the biblical town, Timnah. Since its opening in 1982, the Timnah museum has been the focus of visitors' interest on campus, with thousands of guests registering their appreciation in the museum's guestbook. The display includes photographs, models, maps, and descriptive explanations, together with an impressive representative collection of the cultural artifacts (pottery, figurines, seals, botanical samples, etc.) recovered during the twelve seasons of excavation. Many of the ceramic artifacts on display were restored in the Charles D. Tandy Center for Archaeological Research, which also was funded by the Tandy Foundation. For the very attractive presentation of the artifacts and artwork in the museum, the expedition is indebted to Rachel J. Colvin, who was responsible for the beautiful calligraphy that enhances every display, and Linda Kelm, who directed the formulation of the displays and served as museum curator.

Fig. A.13. A typical seventh century B.C.E. jar in the northern Shephelah.

Fig. A.14. Shoresh Hotel bungalows, the Timnah expedition's camp.

APPENDIX **2** Archaeological Expedition Staff

(1977–1989)

Core Staff

Expedition Director	George L. Kelm
Archaeological Director	Amihai Mazar
Volunteer Recruitment	Linda L. Kelm
Architect/Draughtsman	Ehud Netzer (1977–78),
	Leen Ritmeyer (1979–89)

Supervisory Staff

Area Supervisors

Osnat Misch (1977–79), James Kautz (1977), Ellis Easterly (1977), C. R. Egedy (1977–79), James Hodges (1977), Baruch Brandl (1978–1988), Bracha Goz (1979), Jimmy Albright (1979), Rafi Greenberg (1981), Alon DeGroot (1981), Hannah Brenik (1981), Moi Fleitman (1982–1988), Tommy Brisco (1982–1984), Merilyn Copland (1983–1987, 1989), Daniel Browning (1984–1986), Larry D. Bruce (1984), Gary Huckabay (1985), Dennis Cole (1985), David Maltsberger (1985, 1988–1989), Scott Langston (1989), Michael Bendon (1989), Avi Harash (1989), Nava Panitz-Cohen (1989).

Supervisory Assistants

Bonnie Magness (1977), F. Policastro (1977), Bracha Goz (1978), Y. Gamlieli (1978), Tommy Brisco (1981), Karen Julius (1984), Karen Tasma (1986, 1988), Karen Wharton (1986), John Monson (1986), Scott Langston (1987), David Maltsberger (1987).

Technical Staff

Restorers:	Linda L. Kelm (1977–89), Orah Mazar (1981–89), Osnat Misch-Brandl (1981–82)
Recorders:	Linda L. Kelm (1977), Betty Egedy (1978–79), Barbara Aucoin (1979), Beverly Brooks (1981), Peggy Kinnaird (1982), Helen Thomas (1983), Michael Horne (1984), Delores Mixer (1985–86, 1988–89), Helen Waisgerber (1987)
Assistant Recorder:	Barbara Miley (1985)
Technical Drawing:	Rahel Solar (1981–89), Shani Culiner (1988), Maria Kaplan (1992–94)
Architect Assistant:	Joyce Harris
Section Drawing:	William Waisgerber (1985,1987), Rosmarie Telschow (1985).
Registrars:	Moi Fleitman (1982–88), Nava Panitz-Cohen (1989–95).
Computer Services:	Dan Browning, David Maltsberger, Nahum Apelbaum, Jean Foley, Gad Yagil, Ilan Sharon.
Photographers:	George L. Kelm (1977–89), David Bell (1984), Zeev Radovan, Ilan Sztulman, Gabi Larom; Aerials, Richard Cleave.
Photo Processing:	Harry Mixer (1985–86, 1988–89)
Video Recording:	Greg Danaha (1985), David Ozman (1986), Adria Ozman (1986).

Analysis and Research

Stratigraphy and Iron Age Pottery:	Nava Panitz-Cohen
Osteology:	Brian Hesse
Botany:	Yehudit Dekel, Mordechai Kislev, Uri Baruch
Weights Analysis:	Avraham Eran
Physical Anthropologist:	Baruch Arensburg
Greek Pottery Analysis:	Jodi Magness
Petrographic Analysis:	Yuval Goren
Neutron Activation Analysis:	Joseph Yellin, Jan Gunneweg
Scarabs:	Baruch Brandl
Loom Weights:	Dan Browning
Stone Objects:	Anat Cohen
Metallurgical Analysis:	Sariel Shalev

APPENDIX 3 Sponsorship and Support

The expedition is indebted to many friends and sponsors for contributions to its success. In 1982, the Kaypro Corporation donated a Kaypro 10 computer to the expedition that allowed us to begin the computerization of the cultural data. With the help of the dBase II (and later dBase III PLUS) programs, we developed a program for the manipulation and evaluation of the data, the results of which will be used in the final reports. Timnah was one of the first major expeditions in Israel to apply computer technology to archaeological analysis.

Besides the main sponsoring institutions mentioned in the preface, additional contributions to the expedition were received from the "Friends of the Timnah Expedition." The expedition is grateful and indebted to all who have supported the program financially. Through the auspices of the Institute of Archaeological Research, travel allowances were granted to faculty and student participants and staff appointees for every season of the expedition's program. The Institute also facilitated the work of the archaeological program with the purchase of office equipment and supplies. While many gifts were made in lesser amounts, contributions of $5000 or more came from Mr. and Mrs. F. Howard Walsh, Sr., Fort Worth, Texas ($100,000); Mr. and Mrs. Johnny Heflin, Little Rock, Arkansas; and Professor and Mrs. George L. Kelm.

A Charles D. Tandy Foundation contribution of $100,000 made possible the establishment of the Charles D. Tandy Archaeological Museum, with its collection of artifacts from Timnah and a portrayal of the excavation and cultural history of the site, housed in the Roberts Library on the Southwestern Seminary campus. An additional $100,000 contribution from the Tandy Foundation was designated specifically for an archaeological research center. The Charles D. Tandy Center for Archaeological Research was established in the Fleming wing of the main administration building on the Southwestern Baptist Seminary campus.

The processing of the finds and preparation of the final excavation report since 1992 have been supported by the Philip and Muriel Berman Center for Biblical Archaeology in the Institute of Archaeology of The Hebrew University and by a research grant from the Israel Academy of Sciences. The Institute of Archaeology of The Hebrew University supplied workshop and storage facilities throughout the term of the project. The Israel Antiquities Authority (formerly the Israel Department of Antiquities and Museums) assisted in administrative matters, in the storage of finds from the excavations, and in permitting shipment of finds to the Charles D. Tandy Archaeological Museum in Fort Worth.